The Light Infantry Officer

The Light Infantry Officer

The Experiences of an Officer
of the 43rd Light Infantry
in America During
the War of 1812

John H. Cooke

LEONAUR

The Light Infantry Officer: the Experiences of an Officer of the
43rd Light Infantry in America During the War of 1812
by John H. Cooke

Published by Leonaur Ltd in 2007

Originally published in 1835 in the book:
A Narrative of Events in the South of France and of the Attack on
New Orleans in 1814 and 1815

ISBN: 978-1-84677-342-6 (hardcover)
ISBN: 978-1-84677-341-9 (softcover)

http://www.leonaur.com

Publisher's Notes

In the interests of authenticity, the spellings, grammar and place names used have been retained from the original edition.

The opinions expressed in this book are those of the author and are not necessarily those of the publisher.

Contents

John Cooke Marches On

Those interested in military history often confine themselves to specific periods or theatres of war. This cannot be said of serving soldiers, who go and fight wherever they are ordered.

There are many military memoirs of the Napoleonic period that end at the First Restoration of the Bourbon monarchy, and others that conveniently pick up again to include the fall of Napoleon and Revolutionary France in 1815 and embrace the Waterloo Campaign and its aftermath.

John Cooke's military memoirs were originally published across three volumes, with the middle volume—oddly—shared with two other writers, and in them he told of his experiences in the Peninsular War and the campaign in the South of France. At the end of that campaign, Cooke's regiment, the 43rd Light Infantry, was ordered to America to take part in the closing battles of the War of 1812, in particular the disastrous—for the British—Battle of New Orleans.

Cooke's 'Napoleonic War' experiences have, for the very first time, been recently gathered into a single volume by Leonaur under the title *With the Light Division*. This book will be new to many readers and we believe that this is the way in which most students of the British army of the period would prefer to read about Cooke's adventures.

Those interested in the Napoleonic Wars do not necessarily concern themselves with the War of 1812 or, indeed, wars in India that took place during the Napoleonic period. The Struggle against the French, under the leadership of the Emperor himself, holds a particular fascination. Nevertheless, the War of 1812 has its own interested body of students, and this book will be a revelation to many, since it too appears as a dedicated volume in it own right for the first time in this Leonaur edition.

There will be others who may—with understandable curiosity—just want to learn what happened next to young John Cooke of the 43rd. Here then are the further military experiences of that officer of Light Infantry.

The Leonaur Editors

CHAPTER 1

A New Campaign

Having sojourned three months in England, our battalion, which was the first of the forty-third, was ordered to embark, commanded by Colonel Patrickson, C.B. The second battalion was stationed in the citadel, under Colonel Joseph Wells. We were to form a brigade with the seventh, or Royal Fusiliers, who were already aboard ship for the same destination, the western world.

Accordingly, on the 10th of October, 1814, having congregated on the beach, we were crowded into ships' barges and launches, for the purpose of being put aboard the transport-ships the *Earl Moira*, the *Woodman*, and the *Helen* brig, lying for our reception in Plymouth Sound. The temperature was chilly, and pendent black clouds darkened the atmosphere; but although contrary gusts of winds burst forth and howled at a distance, foreboding the coming storm, yet the embarkation was persisted in. The sails were hoisted and the small craft put off, an undertaking of great danger, as the barges and launches were so jammed with soldiers, loaded with knapsacks and firelocks, as almost to impede the working and steering of the boats.

The first mishap befell a company in a lighter, which drifted upon the rocks amongst the breakers under the hill on which the long-room barracks are situated. The surf broke over the decks of the little bark with terrific violence as she furiously bumped on the ragged rocks, with a probability of every soul perishing at noon-day within a few yards of the shore, and the troops were well nigh washed overboard before any assistance could be afforded, as they could not for some time be extricated from their perilous situation.

The whole of the small craft at length got round St. Nicholas' Island, the wind nearly dead ahead, where we encountered the foaming billows majestically rolling inland, and tossing the boats up and down in a most furious manner, the surf bursting over the sides of the small craft with a loud crash, and the salt spray drenching us to the skin. After some hours' buffeting against the foaming element, we reached the *Helen* brig, the nearest vessel, but she was pitching and rolling to such an excess that the boats were nearly swamped, and it took two hours getting the soldiers up her slippery ladder, particularly those already described, who had been nearly sacrificed at the outset in the lighter, which had struck on the rocks, and were now so benumbed with cold as hardly to be capable of using their limbs.

When on board, everything bore the most comfortless aspect; the dead lights were in the stern windows, and a suffocating smell issued from the close and contracted cabin. Very few soldiers of the whole corps succeeded in getting on board their proper transports, and the rest of the corps were driven or scattered at the mercy of the wind and the waves; some boats were washed ashore at Cawsand, whilst others were forced to seek shelter at Plymouth, heartily sick of this tempestuous day's prelude of a coming voyage to the New World.

For myself, the tossing and violent motion of the launches produced such violent sea-sickness, during the long and difficult operation of getting the men on board the *Helen*, that some naval officers volunteered to convey me again ashore in one of their smaller boats, to cast up my accounts in more comfortable quarters; and even the naval officers, towards the close of this tempestuous day, were sea-sick, and could not keep upon their stomach the clotted cream and other good things of Devonshire.

The following night and day I felt much indisposed with a dry and racking pain in my stomach, and after drinking quantities of tea I was at last fain to apply to Dr. Hair for some medicine; this was the first time I had passed through his hands, or that he had ever administered to my necessities in his professional calling. However, in this his first attempt, the dose proved a total failure, or rather the cramp had laid too strong a hold of my intestines to be removed by a common draught; for, alas! my. guts felt like dried fiddle-strings, and at last I was seized with such violent paroxysms that I dropped down in a small storeroom crammed with beer-barrels and empty bottles, and although rooms affording good accommodation were within a few yards of my place of refuge, it was found impossible to move me.

The empty bottles being therefore scraped into a corner, a mattress was placed under me while rolling about in the most excruciating agony, and for two days it was impossible to remove me, as I continued in a dangerous state. The whole of the first night Dr. Hair tried every remedy he could think of to reduce my torments to some degree of moderation; he poured hot diluents down my throat, stuck his lancet into me, bringing away forty-eight ounces of blood at the first bleeding, and tried various other remedies too numerous to mention. At length I heard him say that I could not hold out much longer. The renowned Dr. Hair was resolved, however, that I should not depart this life easily, so without more ado he tore off my shirt, and calling out for a cauldron of hot water, and splitting a blanket in twain, he immersed it into the smoking cauldron, and having wrung it out he placed it on the soles of my feet and so up to my chin. This being repeated several times I fell into a slumber, and after some hours' repose awoke free from pain, but as yellow as saffron, and, without using a technical phrase, I had passed a gallstone, and the deep yellow hue tinted my frame and countenance for some days.

Dr. Hair pronounced me to be unfit to take a voyage across the Atlantic, the great probability being that, in the event of a second attack, I should sink under it, and my carcase would be thrown overboard, and become food for the fishes. I was, therefore, ordered to be left behind my dear comrades, some of whom went, for honour and glory, to meet more violent deaths, and to be buried without coffins. *Vive la Gloire!*

On my being landed, I was consigned to the care of the second battalion, in the citadel, though I properly belonged to the first. This was somewhat odd, for when I formerly belonged to the second I had joined the first, in Spain, or rather in rocky Portugal, and I shall never forget having offended a doctor at Salamanca.

Perhaps I may have intruded my ailments on the reader at a greater length than is expedient for one so humble as myself, and walking as I do with so many men of aches and pains. But as the great majority of travellers bring themselves forward in a similar manner, how can one forget self; and, in honest truth, it seems to be the most straightforward way of doing the thing effectually. For whether we puff ourselves or get others to do the like for us, comes, in the sequel, to one and the same thing.

As for doctors I always speak of them with some caution, knowing that there is a time to come when mortality cannot escape their prescriptions any more than they, at the last gasp, who cry to a fellow doctor, "Bleed me no more—drench me no more—and let me die in peace; the system is exhausted."

The celebrated Dr. Kitchener, with whom I was intimately acquainted, assured me that no conscientious man could be a physician, and, owing to those feelings, he had given up the profession, wishing to live and die an honest man; and, upon coming to a property, he accordingly pitched the doctor of physic and the apothecary into the pestle and mortar. But, now that the physician and the apothecary are united in one person, it may explode the old practice of puffing one another, according to Dr. Kitchener's asseverations.

Dr. Kitchener, indeed, was a real character in every sense of the word, both from his singularity and accomplishments. William Kitchener, M.D. is well entitled to a place in any man's book, and the outlines of his tall person both in dress and movement were well worthy the pencil of an artist. I have often partaken of his ragouts and excellent fare; his house was fitted up with every comfort and convenience for the use of the infirm or the indolent, and his dining-room could boast of more than one easy chair to draw round the bright blaze of his cheerful fireside of a winter evening. His wines were of much variety, and of the choicest qualities, both in respect to age and good keeping. He drank little himself, but his guests suited their own palates in quantity as well as quality.

Among other things he was a stargazer, and I cannot forget his keeping me one fine starlight night looking through his telescope, when I wished for the more comfortable chimney-corner, for my finger-ends and my nose waxed cold; but this was his hobby at that time, and there was no getting away; I was fain, therefore, to make a virtue of necessity, and bear the chilly examination of Mars, Venus, and the Milky Way, with philosophical patience. The ethereal arch expanded in the immensity of space canopied us over with a vast blue concave, studded with brilliant and twinkling gems; but it was lost upon me, and I longed for the chimney-corner, for my philosophical genius was as yet latent, and I had no turn whatever for objects of astronomical enquiry.

Besides which, the doctor's music in his back parlour was much more acceptable to me. His piano possessed two rows of keys, and other jingling accompaniments, sounding, when the pedals were touched by the foot, like tambourine, triangle, and a description of trumpet. The doctor did not possess what may be termed a fine voice, but rather an acquired one, but it was of a good bass tone, and extremely agreeable. His selection of songs and music was in excellent taste, and he struck the keys of this instrument with great power and rapidity of finger; he shook his head and shoulders, and sang and played with much apparent satisfaction and glee, the more particularly when singing Dibdin's sea songs.

Towards myself he was very familiar in his conversation, talking on all subjects without reserve; and were I to retail all he told me of the drug and the lancet, half the faculty would be up in arms against me. His pleasant description of the ladies' mixtures was not the least droll article of his medicinal budget.

The worthy doctor contended that cleaning the teeth of a morning was pernicious; that the proper time for brushing them was at night, to cleanse their interstices from the particles of food lodged in certain cavities, or in unsound teeth, after the usual meals. The operation of brushing being performed, he maintained that, during sleep, nature covered them with a sort of coat for their preservation during the day. Into this disquisition I will not enter, doctors differ, as it is not my province to go further into the subject than merely to state his opinion.

This celebrated character always wore blue or green

spectacles, and possessed only one eye. I once met him in a ramble in Middlesex, with a large bamboo cane sloped over his left shoulder, and the ferule end stuck through the knuckle of a ham which rested upon his back, while in the other hand he held a scroll of music of his own composition, which he was merrily distributing to those friends whom he might chance to meet as he trudged along the highway; of course I came in for a share of his favours. This eccentricity was acted to the life, and charmingly carried on to his own infinite amusement. At this time he was in the enjoyment of an ample income, and the circumstance occurred years before he wrote his book of advice for the benefit of the dining gentry, who expect a well covered mahogany every day of their lives.

Like a young colt I have somewhat gambolled and strayed away from my subject, but this is no matter, and gives variety to the scene. Dr. Kitchener's assertions do not hold good in regard to the red-coated doctors; as for them there is no fee, and accordingly it was remarkable how sparing they were of drugs and draughts, and the comparatively few doses of medicine which were given to a whole regiment, in comparison with what would be administered to a like number of civilians, under the care of what are called private practitioners. This, therefore, is a good opportunity of thanking Dr. Hair, who, putting aside his professional routine, and tucking up his shirtsleeves, went to work like a man.

Although Dr. Hair had promulgated his veto that I should be left behind, my friend Æolus, the god of winds, bellowed forth, "No, I ordain otherwise!" and *malgré* angry masters of vessels, and their whistling for a fair wind, he blew in their teeth, and rolled his angry waves into the Sound, tossing big ships, little ships, transports, and men-of-war up and down like cockle-shells.

CHAPTER 2

I Set Sail at Last

At the end of a fortnight, the 26th of October, my second battalion servant, while lighting my fire early in the morning, told me, thinking I was to stop behind, that the wind was at last fair, that the fleet was preparing to sail, and that blue peter was hoisted at the mastheads. At this intelligence I jumped out of bed, bustled about, got my war-kit together, and made for the beach as fast as my tottering legs would carry me. There I only found one boat; the terms were rather extravagant, but there was no redress; stepping into it, therefore, and pushing off, I soon descried the *Helen* brig; her stern loaded with greens and cabbages, a sure criterion by which to find a troopship, and after being hauled up her sides, was sincerely hailed by my companions, who had now gained their sea-legs. The anchor was already hoisted, the sails were unfurled, and with a fair breeze the vessels ploughed the deep, and scudded before the wind, convoyed by the *Vengeur* of seventy-four guns.

Breakfast was on the table, and ship-biscuit. "Ship-biscuit! the first day of leaving harbour," I exclaimed; "what! not a loaf of bread on board?" which was indeed too true. What a caterer! and my stomach had hardly regained sufficient tone to endure the well-known smell of the biscuit-bag.

Two officers belonging to the second battalion had stolen away without leave, and came aboard our two-masted brig to share in the further toils of "flood and field;" and we now mustered no fewer than eleven individuals, including two medical officers, in the small cabin, which contained two narrow berths on each side, and also two dark holes, with doorways, bearing the title of *state-cabins,* from whence issued, for the benefit of our nasal faculties, an effluvium which was a mixture of the most offensive and sickening compounds.

Five persons being still without berths, they were accommodated at night with *two cots,* slung under the skylight; the three others lay on the floor; consequently there was hardly an inch unoccupied of this den, which measured eight feet in breadth and six in length. Fortunately a more good-tempered set of persons could not have been congregated together; one of them, whose height was more than six feet, could not take up his berth on the middle plank of the cabin until the fire was extinguished of a night, for when stretched out at full length he was forced to cram his feet under the grate.

Although each of us had subscribed twenty-two pounds for articles of sea-stock, such as pigs, poultry, sheep, hams, porter, wine, and food for the livestock, yet, owing to bad management, the trickery of the hucksters, and the contracted stowage of the vessel, everything was mixed up together in such a disorderly way, that we scarcely enjoyed a well-served meal during our long voyage. The moist sugar became damp, and found its way into the butter-tub; the salt water trickled into the biscuit and flour barrels; corks flew from the porter-bottles, and the *vin de Bordeaux,* which had been brought from France, fermented and turned as sour as *verjuice*; the hay for the sheep was soaked with the rain, impregnated by salt-water, and rotting in the jolly-boat, where our pigs and sheep were stowed away; the latter, from exposure, soon became in such a sickly condition, that we were obliged to kill and eat them, to prevent their dying a natural death.

Amongst other pleasant things, it was suspected that the brig had a hole in her side, for as she tossed to and fro, the soldiers on watch were constantly called to stand to the pumps; but with all these accumulated drawbacks, we were as happy as any set of people could be under similar circumstances.

Staff-doctor Ryan and myself amused ourselves by playing chess; but, as if our patience was to be put to the rack in every possible shape, one day, when the blast whistled through the rigging and the close-reefed topsails, the vessel gave a sudden lurch, and before I could reach the hen-coop, I had the inexpressible satisfaction, if so it may be called, of seeing my set of chessmen slide overboard into the foaming deep. It was in vain that I hung over the gunwale to look for them, the bubble in the frothing vortex had swallowed them up—they were gone, irretrievably gone.

Such a loss was not to be endured without putting our ingenuity to the rack how to supply the deficiency, and within a fortnight we shaped out a fresh set of chessmen from pasteboard, which were painted to represent knights of old and men-at-arms on one opposing side, and the scimitar and turbaned heads of the crescent on the other; these figures, being stuck up in wooden stands, were flanked by dignified viziers and embattled castles.

The chessmen were no sooner completed than the staff-doctor Ryan and myself again recommenced our rivalry, and were so equally matched, that, should he lose two or three games in succession, he would pace the deck for the rest of the day in an abstracted mood, and as every trifling circumstance or change of countenance is noticed at sea, the officers would banter him; but when the victor, he would feign the same moody manner, as if unsuccessful, to deceive these plagues. Often while ruminating on the loss of a game he would endeavour to button the lower part of his tartan jacket, and when he succeeded in closing it, looked cheerful, and his plagues said, while encircling him:

"Ah! we see you have been the conqueror to day!"

"How?"

"Why, you have buttoned your jacket, and no longer swelling with vexation."

With these chessmen we played ninety-five games during the voyage: these and other pastimes were resorted to, which beguiled the tedious days on the Atlantic ocean.

The frequent changes of weather from *fair to foul,* and from *foul to fair,* at sea, form part of the wonders of a nautical life. In the evening the sky encircles the mariner, with a transparent canopy tinged by the brightest colours, and the inflamed and crimsoned day-lamp of heaven sinks into the mighty deep, whose transparent waters shine like polished steel, or with the smoothness of the brightest mirror; all is hushed, the sails hang loosely, or flap at intervals in the gentle evening breeze; the ship lies like a log on the briny element, and the bubbling waters at her bow is the only indication that she floats with the current.

The sailors amuse themselves by dancing or playing various games. The passenger forgets his longings for the promised land, and lounges on the deck inhaling the cool and refreshing air, which, with gentle murmurs, flirts at intervals, by fanning the drooping pendant. At midnight the unwilling mariner retires to his confined berth, impressed with the soft tranquillity of the scene, and sinks into sweet slumbers, from which, perhaps, he suddenly awakes, amid the storm, with palpitating heart, and involuntarily seizes hold of the sides of his berth to save himself from being flung from his nest on to the cabin floor; a violent motion agitates the bark every plank is strained, the vessel cracks with appalling noises as if about to be shivered or split in twain, and the trampling and rustling of footsteps over his head leads to fearful conclusions; the vessel rolls from side to side, she rises, and then spins downwards with terrific rapidity into the foaming abyss, as if engulfed, and swallowed up in the settling or gurgling of the waters; she again plunges, the wind howls, all the sails are close reefed, the frail bark is running under bare poles before the wind, and hurrying through the angry deep with strange velocity.

After some weeks sailing we reached the latitudes of the trade-winds, which continued light and baffling for six days; the commodore of the *Vengeur* hoisted signals for the masters of transports to go on board, to ask their opinions on the subject. The atmosphere was now warm and genial, and the huge monsters of the deep were seen spouting up the water afar off like cascades, and the *flying fishes* frequently dropped on the decks of our vessel; the largest I saw was about two-thirds the size of a herring, their wings are of a texture representing the finest gauze: these fishes fly rapidly above the surface of the water for twenty or thirty yards and sometimes more; one of them fell on the deck of the *Helen*, but the moment their wings become dry, they drop helplessly into the water.

The day we crossed the equator, or tropical line, it was intimated to us that it was a usual custom to present a certain number of gallons of spirits to the sailors, which was readily acquiesced in, to avoid going through the disagreeable ordeal of an introduction to Neptune. I don't know how this accomplished exhibition is practiced in larger ships, therefore I can only describe the ceremony as it took place on board our two-masted brig. A boat was placed on the deck half filled with bilge-water, on the sharp edge of which sat a sailor, which must have been very far from an easy position; he was first lathered with a tar-brush, and then shaved with a ragged iron rusty hoop, and from his wriggling about seemed to feel intense pain; but during the operation he was from time to time cheered up, by being told that as soon as the operation was completed he should see Neptune. But just before the deity of the ocean was supposed to come on board, the poor wretch was covered over the head and shoulders with a sack, when the god appeared on deck, in green, with a horrible mask resembling some imaginary sea-monster, with sea-weeds dangling from every part of his figure, and the deity having bellowed forth certain expressions, the sailor was then pushed violently backwards from the edge of the boat over head and ears into the bilge water, and while struggling to extricate himself out of the sack, which he at last effected with considerable difficulty, and quite exhausted, as black as a tinker, while gasping for breath, and well-nigh suffocated, and reeling from side to side, so soon as he was able to unclose an eye, behold! Neptune stood before him, when he was drenched by the bystanders with buckets of salt water, and unmercifully belaboured with swab's. The whole affair was brutal in the extreme, and we all turned away quite disgusted at the ferocious process.

A few days after this occurrence, while sitting round the rollers of the cabin table just after dinner, we heard a bustling of feet on the deck, and the cry of "a man overboard!" The vessel was scudding along under a gentle breeze, but in three minutes the soldier was left some hundred yards in her wake; fortunately he was an excellent swimmer, and succeeded in taking off his grey great coat in the water, and kept himself afloat until a boat was lowered and rowed to his assistance, and got him safely on board little the worse for his ducking. One night a soldier disappeared from the vessel, and was never afterwards heard of, and it was supposed that he fell out of the chains during the night.

Amongst other circumstances a soldier-shoemaker, of literary attainments, was in the habit of writing a letter for a penny, or a cut of tobacco of equal value, to the different friends or relatives of soldiers; and for the more ready despatch of business, the writer kept a few uniform copies ready written and folded for all occasions, excepting the heading, a space being left blank to answer for the Christian names of the male or female gender, as the case might be.

It was truly amusing, when he was so commissioned, for a bystander to observe the anxious eye of the would-be dictator, who was always commanded to be gone from the elbow of the supposed compositor acting under the dictation which might have been given him beforehand, who in place of using his ink-horn, now filled to the brim with gunpowder and water or any other sable mixture at hand, would quietly smoke his pipe or mend an old shoe, at the same moment a peculiar happy sneer stealing across a naturally expressive face. And although more than once it required considerable dexterity to deceive the untutored correspondents in a closely-packed vessel, yet the shoemaker usually contrived to do so. And although the greater portion of the men in the vessel might hold epistolary correspondence written alike word for word ready for delivery by the first home-bound vessel, yet this shoemaker kept up the deception by affixing his thumbnail on chewed biscuit, which, when dry, secured the contents from the eye of curiosity, and answered in lieu of wafers.

There was little chance of the holders of these copies, taken from the same sheet, comparing notes, as in the first place they could not read, nor was it likely they would attempt to open their family affairs, supposed to be in black and white, to those less gifted than the shoemaker, who by the means described was the sole repository of half the secrets of those on board, and not one word of all that had been confided to his keeping had he ever attempted to put to paper. He was an orator as well as a writer, for while reading the supposed compositions, he would repeat or interlard whole sentences for the edification of his auditor, which only existed in his own fancy.

All this we were told and likewise knew it to be the fact; and I heard him once say to a man, while measuring a fine figure from head to foot, accompanying his words with a look of the most utter scorn, "Go along, you fool! What's the girl's name? That's all I want to know; do you think I don't know better what to say to her than you do?"

This athletic shoemaker once declared, while falling in for an attack without his knapsack, he was so used to it that it felt like part and parcel of himself, and without its additional weight he could not walk steadily. And this man had fired away, in battle, ball-cartridge enough to load an ass.

CHAPTER 3

We Reach the Caribbean

At the expiration of six weeks' sailing, and without once seeing, during our voyage, the outlines of any land, save in imagination from the peculiar formation of clouds on the horizontal line, we at length came in sight of Martinico and Dominico, two West-India islands. The day was charming, and our spirits were highly exhilarated at the view of these mountainous islands; the deep blue waters of the ocean were only agreeably agitated, the crests of the rolling waves were garnished with white and resplendent foam, and the silvery refraction from the sun danced on the curls of the sportive waves with flirting cheerfulness.

What with land and water combined, the scene, with half-closed eyes, resembled a moving panorama, the vessel moving along in a parallel course to the land, at the rate of eight knots the hour, one way, while the rocks in one grand mass seemed to recede in an opposite direction, and in the like agreeable delusion I have often indulged, the vessel skimming along the surface of the water.

Time hangs so heavy at sea that since we had left England an age seemed to have elapsed, and the lofty blue mountains towering out of the waters acting on the fancy like awakening from a dream.

The *Vengeur* was about eight miles ahead, and having

just veered round, for the purpose of passing between the islands of Martinico and Dominico in this position, her broadside facing our bows, with her sails spread out, she resembled a large goose in the midst of a flock of goslings, the white sails of the rest of the convoy nestling close under her outstretched wings. But the poor *Helen* was totally thrown out and had no claim to be counted as one of the flock, for she was all behind, her bows pummelling and tossing up the briny waters as though she was performing a prodigy in sailing.

At this time a large white sail was descried far astern, apparently carried along in a sheet of continuous foam, and in this way sweeping along the waters parallel to our wake, as if in a vast hurry, for never did I see one sail gain on another with such velocity. A constant white foam shrouded and disguised the outlines of this vessel from the vision, the water rising with a prodigious impetus, and falling like a thousand cascades, and in this way gaining on us rapidly; and when within a mile or two astern we told the master that this strange sail looked ominous. But with too much self-confidence he took upon himself to pronounce, with true nautical and most infallible assurance, that she was only some small coaster.

The master often expressed deep surprise at the unusual slow sailing of the *Helen* while crossing the Atlantic; and it was still suspected that she had a hole in her bottom, or some of her timbers damaged, from her constantly making so much water, and the men being obliged to stand so often to the pumps; and these suspicions were too soon verified.

The strange sail had now gained on us considerably, and the master had been advised to be on his guard, but without effect; while I for one vehemently endeavoured to impress on him that precautionary measures was only being on the right side; he thought otherwise, and would not give ear to the proffered advice to send below for some of the small arms, which had been stowed away, to be placed in the hands of the unarmed soldiers. Whether the master disliked the trouble, or really thought there was no danger to be apprehended, he still obstinately persisted that preparations of a hostile nature were useless. But when the vessel, crowding all sail, was within five or six hundred yards of our stern, the master took the glass from his eye, and turning pale, said, in a hurried and frightened manner, "I now fear she is an enemy and going to run aboard us."

This was not the first time in my life that I had seen proper precautions jeered at, and the very people who did so the very first to lose their intellects at the critical moment when all energies are most wanted; and the schooner was nearly alongside, when now came the odious confusion—officers running down to the cabin to seize their swords, and a few soldiers scrambling upon deck with ten or a dozen uncleaned muskets, all that could be laid hold of, and without having time to get at their ammunition; a pretty joke forsooth: his Majesty's troops, muffled up in grey great coats, reduced perhaps to fight with their fists against cutlass, boarding pike, and pistol, for the decks of this vessel were crowded with a group of piratical independent-looking fellows, of all sorts of complexions, while carelessly lounging in every possible posture, some leaned over the gunwale, whilst others stood erect with arms folded on her decks, or akimbo.

These men wore red and striped shirts; many of their sleeves tucked above the elbows of their brawny arms; their heads cased in various coloured handkerchiefs or hairy caps, and other outlandish gear; hardly one of these piratical-looking fellows wore a jacket, owing to the genial warmth of the atmosphere. At first they hailed us in French through a hoarse speaking-trumpet, a language we pretended not to understand; they then questioned us in English. But finding that we were only a transport, they took no further notice, and ploughed through the water to reconnoitre the body of the convoy. She appeared to be pierced, or her false ports were painted to represent her as carrying twelve or fourteen guns, and we kept our eyes on her, expecting every instant that she intended to haul off and throw long shots at us, which undoubtedly would have been the case had we been a prize worth having.

Her commander could hardly have pictured to his imagination the utter confusion on board of us. To be sure two or three of us were armed, and no doubt all ready to fight—but it must have been with fists. Whenever I think of this circumstance, I am in a rage, for I never witnessed so much listless stupidity in my whole life; some running up the companion ladders to see what was the matter, and others running down to search for bayonets or some offensive weapons, so that one party obstructed the other; and although no attempt was made on us, it is very unsatisfactory to reflect that most probably not being worth having was the only reason that we were not made a prize of, and the *Helen* with her living cargo scuttled and sent to the bottom for soundings before her time.

In the afternoon we passed between the islands of Martinico and Dominico, the former being remarkable as the birthplace of the captivating and amiable Josephine, the first wife of, and subsequently Napoleon's empress.

The coast of Dominico is also celebrated for the victory gained near that island by Admiral Rodney over the Compte de Grasse, in June 1787. The youthful Prince William Henry, Duke of Clarence, was present at this sea-fight as an inferior officer in the royal navy, and now seated on the throne of his royal ancestors as King William the Fourth of Great Britain and Ireland, and who proved himself the royal patron of the immortal Nelson, which is enough to grace his Majesty, whether as a king or a man, beyond all manner of doubt, to the lasting and deep gratitude of his subjects. Captain Sir Charles Douglas, at Rodney's victory, won great honours as master of the fleet, as being one of the first to propose breaking the enemies' line of battle, a bold manoeuvre, which was also afterwards executed by Nelson at the Nile and Trafalgar.

Diminico and Martinico are about the centre of the Antilles, a string of beautiful islands which stretch from the Spanish main in the form of a crescent towards St. Domingo, which islands in a manner divide the mighty waters of the Atlantic ocean from the more circumscribed limits of the Caribbean Sea. When within the Caribbean Sea the spectacle was truly charming; the two islands rising out of the polished and dark blue waters, and the outlines of these colossal mountains tinted with every light and shade, and their lofty pinnacles capped with the clear atmosphere of these regions. The dark blue sea was only gently agitated, the polished waves, crested with foam like plumes of ostrich feathers; and afar off was seen a British man-of-war, her chequered broadside looking like a chess board.' A warm breeze passed our faces, and the motion of the vessel was so gentle, that we felt as if floating on the waters of perpetual sunshine.

In these latitudes all at once the serenity of the heavens is changed, the tropical luminary is hid behind, the rolling black clouds, the thunder roars, the elements are of liquid fire, and the rains descend in a sheet of water, the mighty earthquake shakes the foundations of the islands, and the mountains open into yawning chasms; churches and houses are blown down by the whirlwind, or are swallowed up by the earthquake; blacks, whites, *creóles*, and *pic-a-ninnies*, are engulfed in the bowels of the earth, buried alive, or are swept away by the mighty torrents, roaring down the sides of the mountain-ravines or watercourses; whole plantations are destroyed, swept off the face of nature; trees are rent in twain, and torn up by the roots and whisked into the air, with men, women, and children; the hurricane rages with unabated fury, and the concatenation of awful noises are as if the day of retribution for all sinners was come to sum up their offences.

The solitary vessel is lifted up and down by the waves of the sea, and tossed hither and thither; the waves, racing, howling, and tumbling one over the other, and pounding the sides of the bark, which is going up and down in a hurry, over and under the mad waves. The frail bark is no longer manageable, and is either dashed upon the rocks, or bumping its bottom out amongst the hideous roar of the outrageous breakers, or probably is scuttled by the electric fluid piercing her timbers, and driving her to the bottom of the sea. Now, whether the sails are shivered to shreds, or the ship and crew are doomed to be drowned by a water-spout, or struck by a thunder-bolt, signifies little when the catastrophe comes, attended in such a whirlwind.

And those that dread the cholera in England, let them just stand at the gang-way of a ship, when the elements are discomposed by a hurricane, and the sea is a rage. If they do not wish themselves in England again, with all the chances of the cholera, I am no prophet!

But the hurricane is exhausted and dies a natural death, and nature smiles as before, and the distant lands and seas resume their pristine beauties, and the vertical sun glances merrily upon the purple waters of these uncertain seas.

All these accompaniments may be calculated upon in the Caribbean seas; therefore when we partake of West Indian sweets at home, let us think of her sours abroad.

But let me gather together my wandering thoughts, that

I am still on board the *Helen*. A gentle breeze wafted us through the purple waters of the Caribbean sea; and in this manner for days we scudded before the wind, passed within sight of the Island of St. Domingo, or Hispaniola, without forgetting the great massacre committed by the blacks a few years before, upon the heads of the French, their former masters. Thence coasting along the shores of the Island of Jamaica; and, although we had heard much about curries, pangaree, spices, and aromatic plants, still nothing of the sort at this time came within our grasp, or within the scent of our olfactory sensations.

The temperature was now exceedingly hot, and certain hits were thrown out, one to the other, in a jocular way, as table-talk, of incidental malaria, the black vomit, and the last remains of mortality being consigned ashore to the claws of the land-crabs. And, by the way, it would be worse than inattention, on the part of the voyager, did he fail to replenish his literary and philanthropic store, while passing these latitudes, the hotbed of slavery, without remembering the name of William Wilberforce, (so long the honourable member for Yorkshire,) the strenuous advocate for the emancipation of his more sable brethren, Africa's victims of slavery, consigned to the whip of the capricious and ruthless overseer. And let us also breathe an inward response to the manes of those white men who have perished in the cause of humanity on and near the coast of Guinea.

In the middle of December, one night, we stood off Port Royal, with the hope of landing at that place the following morning; but no, the morrow only showed the sails still bent before the wind; the weather was now so hot that we threw off all our clothing, and paced the deck in our shirt-sleeves and duck trousers, without stockings or neck-cloths. The wind was still propitious, and gentle gales carried us past Jamaica and Nigril Bay; the sky was serene, but we longed to cast anchor, but continued our course five hundred miles along the shores of the Island of Cuba, and at last bade farewell to Cape Antonio, thus making about five thousand miles, without taking down canvass, but there was no cessation of sailing.

CHAPTER 4

The Gulf of Mexico

After entering the Gulf of Mexico, one fine day, we saw the back of a huge whale above the surface of the water, about one hundred and fifty yards ahead, or rather on the larboard bow of the creaking vessel, which slowly rose and fell on the long swell of the translucent waters. To describe the bulk and the monstrous broad dark back of this *spermaceti* whale, which rose a very considerable height above the surface of the water, I will not attempt to do, from a fear that it might be supposed that my eye magnified its dimension? I can only say, at first sight, it looked like a vessel turned bottom upwards, and in this way rising slowly above the surface of the water. Many others now in existence saw it as well as myself. And an officer, who was not a little proud of a well-cleaned rifle, bounded down the companion-ladder into the cabin, reappeared on the deck, and taking aim at this mighty whale—*twang* went the rifle, whether the ball rebounded from its back, or whether he missed it altogether I know not, but I do know that the splash from the ball falling into the water, some way beyond the whale, was visible to us all.

The leviathan of the deep then raised and expanded its broad fins to their full extent, and the huge broad back of the monster slowly sank into the unfathomed depths of its briny element. The countenance of the shooter portrayed keen chagrin, no doubt, at the bare idea of missing a whale. The group of silent and smiling spectators casting significant looks at each other, at once splitting into twos and threes, and politely turning away their heads, leaned over the gunwales of the vessel to give way to their shaking sides and most exceeding mirth, as the tears of merriment were forced from their eyes, which sprinkled and were mixed in the long swell of the ocean's waters.

Twelve days after passing Port Royal, we were in the middle of the Gulf of Mexico. The atmosphere was piercing cold, and it was necessary to cloak and to stamp our feet on the decks, to keep ourselves warm; the blast was now howling, and the frail barks rolling and dashing through the foaming billows. The bad stock of provisions were almost exhausted, but enough of plums had been retained to make a plum-pudding on Christmas day. In all climes and in all places, we never failed to do honour to this day of devotion and feasting. The staff-doctor, Ryan, suffered much from an internal complaint, causing a swelling of the belly, which was externally evident from the large size of it at times, and this disease eventually carried him off.

The worthy doctor was much esteemed amongst us, possessing most kind, gentlemanly manners, and acted as a sort of umpire withal; he held under lock and key a dozen of wine, for the use of the public weal, in case of sickness; and I will affirm that these twelve bottles of port caused him more pain and anxiety than is readily explained. When our stock of wine had been long exhausted these twelve bottles of wine were the eternal theme of daily conversation as soon as the dinner-cloth was removed; and it was an exquisite study to observe his conscience struggling against good nature, as we exclaimed, as with one voice, Doctor! Doctor! we are all sick, feel our pulse.

The following morning a stiff breeze blew, and the sea looked as if it was literally boiling, for a steam floated on the surface of the waves, such as I had never before witnessed.

In a few days we had traversed the Gulf of Mexico.

CHAPTER 5

The Coast of America

The master of the *Helen* was a civil well-behaved north-countryman, and hearing we were badly off, brought to light a fine ham, and a large brown pan of potatoes, which he presented to us; and a very acceptable present it was, as we had been reduced to salt junk for some days, and our stock of vegetables had been long exhausted. It will be needless to add that, without loss of time or any useless preliminaries, we set to work to demolish this offering. The Anglo-Saxon or the more modern Anglo-Norman has been accused as the exclusive lover of the more substantial good things of this sublunary sphere; but from all the experience which has come within my optic scope, this gastronomic gift seems to be so equally poised between the respective champions of the rose, the shamrock, and the thistle, as to amalgamate their masticating propensities into a most decided neck-and-neck dead heat

Ship-board is the place of all others for arguments, and for finding out the dispositions of people so often put to the trial, and for ever jostling one another for want of space, or the more active amusements on shore; and I have often joined in and enjoyed much mirth and laughter at some of the vehement and feudal-like arguments and discussions between the Caledonian and Hibernian companions of "voyage and travel:" and as the respective champions of either country were equal in point of numbers, nothing could equal the droll and far-fetched arguments on both sides, for the ascendancy of *clan, province, or country.*

When the weather was moderate, these wrangles generally began as the various individuals stowed themselves away; and from their berths or queer places of rest, heads here and there popped up and down as the debates went on; one raised the night-cap from hindering the sight of a right or left eye, the doors of the two holes or state cabins were hastily opened for the ensconced persons to get a word in.

The highlanders accused the lowlanders of being neutrals, and worse than *common Englishmen;* the lowlanders retorted on the highlanders, calling them the bare-a——d cattle stealers from the mountains; the Hibernians protested that the Scots were renegades from the green isle, and vice versa; the Caledonians swearing that they were no way connected with the Milesians who were nothing more than pirates from the coast of Spain, or some tribe of Eskimos from the frozen regions, which had been thrown into the bogs of Ireland by some convulsion of the elements, or tossed across the Atlantic ocean before Columbus discovered America. The Hibernian vociferating from berth, chair, and table, that the Scotch were the refuse of the Goths or Vandals, or more likely a few rank red-haired Norwegian fishermen, who had lost their own shores in the dark, and were cast away on the shore of Caledonia; and that these dunderheaded boors, crossed by the more pure Milesian blood, had now reached some degree of civilization, being taught at Sunday-schools to read and write by St. Patrick, or by some other of the Irish and enlightened saints.

The 31st of December the American coast was announced from the mast-head; the atmosphere was tinged with greyish clouds, forming a canopy, which cast a peculiar light over the calm expanse of the sea, which shone in perspective like the brightest quicksilver, and the tufted tops of the dark firtrees were the first objects we distinguished as it were rising just above the surface of the bright water on the horizontal line.

As the vessel neared these trees, their appearance still deceived the naked eye, resembling dark clouds floating on the water, and were well worthy the pencil of the artist. By degrees the outlines of these trees showed themselves more distinctly, and with the assistance of the telescope the straight stems of the longer fir-trees were seen to emerge by degrees, and looked as if growing out of the water. And as I have stated before, that in Europe officers were sent to look out for wood and water, but now both seemed united, and hour after hour this enormous forest became more distinct, and at length we obtained a full view of the vast and continuous flats of Louisiana, which forms the delta or left bank of the mouth or mouths of the mighty Mississippi river.

In the afternoon the *Helen*, drawing little water, lay to within the bank or bar, which extends right across the mouth of this river. The weather was still serene, and hardly a breath of air disturbed the tranquillity of the waters, which still presented a smooth surface, and where the current of the river united with the Gulf of Mexico, there was a bubbling ripple, about a foot in breadth, extending in a straight line as far as the eye could scan; and immediately on one side of this singular ripple the water was of a fine sea-green, and on that of the river it was of a light sand, or rather tinged of a clay colour. We lay-to for some hours, looking out for the British fleet from the Chesapeake.

The *Helen* brig, of one hundred and sixty tons, moved slowly round like a duck upon a mill-pond, and was the only vessel I saw within the bar of the Mississippi, as she drew comparatively little water when classed with the other transports.

The last day of December was drawing to a close, and at twilight not a vestige of land was to be seen save the cypress and the pine-trees growing out of the swamps which verged the left bank of the river, the banks on both sides of this river were not perceptible to us owing to its width, and may be termed artificial, and they abut farther into the Gulf of Mexico year after year, which are formed by the condensed trunks of trees that float down the river becoming fixtures, as they are closely wedged together, like rafts, the apertures or interstices of these trunks being filled up with a composition of reeds, slime, roots of trees, and mud, which when united, in time, forms a sort of foothold for man thereon to construct a log house, who acts as pilot to vessels navigating up the Mississippi.

The wonderful progress of this prodigious flood from many rivers which runs through the wilds of America, bringing down in its overwhelming torrents, at one fell swoop, whole tracts of forest trees, both root and branch, which are undermined or melted away from its banks as well as the Missouri and other rivers.

Some of these ponderous trees, as they are whirled round and round in the eddies of currents, often stick at the bottom of the deep Mississippi, their enormous limbs or branches bristling above or below the surface of its turbid waters, like the skeleton of an abattis, which renders its navigation both difficult and dangerous, as these branches frequently stave in and make holes in the bottoms of vessels that are propelled by the wind, its stream likewise running at the rate of four miles the hour.

Calculating, in the revolutions of time, how many carcasses of the cultivators of the sugar-cane, the cotton-tree, the tobacco-plant, or the rice-crop, have been doomed, before the expiration of the natural life of man, to float down this river, either above or below its surface, would be enormous.

The endemics of these vast regions of swamps, which are subject to the additional heat of a tropical sun, strongly reminds me of the rotten fevers and agues in August, September, October, and November, imbibed amongst the dykes of Walcheren and adjacent islands in Europe, where Great Britain lost so many soldiers in 1809, within a short distance of her own shores.

At the mouth of the river Mississippi desolation reigns around, nor was there within the scope of our vista any signs of animation, not even a bird, nor any busy thing, save ourselves: as the evening closed, description expires on the face of these waters, and the mantle of a cloudy evening encircling the smooth sea-green and the vast expanse of turbid water of this river.

On board the *Helen*, I take upon myself the more especially to select three officers, because when the toils of war or the absence of wounds permitted it, we were always in the situation of messmates, with an unanimity of resolve and good fellowship not excelled; and ten years' service was pretty well to try its unity of purpose. We had all put on the scarlet coat or jacket, at from fourteen to sixteen years old, and all had received a liberal education, coming out of the scholastic shell before our time.

My first chum was a Marlowite, and told many stories of the Royal Military College most entertaining, and its correct professors, of serious aspect and glove of doe-skin white as the lily. The second studied under a doctor of divinity in Devonshire; was not always victorious at combats, but a good drubbing did not deter his trying the same victor again. The third was intended for a doctor of theology, but somehow or other a spoke was thrust into the wheel of divinity, and found him in a red jacket, with white facings, at fifteen, figuring at the battle of Vimiera, the youngest of three brothers in that field. He would relax into the most joyful laughter at his own stories, which were so good as to make an apology to Chesterfield quite unnecessary. But his great delight was to describe, while at Westminster, his first sufferings us a fag, and all the vile and unjust torments inflicted upon him, enough to make a galley-slave turn pale; and when he rose to the high estate of task-master, how amply he repaid his fags with compound interest for all he had endured, declaring how he would thrash one fag of a cold winter's morning, if the tea-kettle was not boiling to a moment, or make the back of another echo as from the bowels of a cavern, if the toast was not well browned, although the fag had hardly fire enough to bake a wafer. But the recital given with the most glee was about a fowling-piece used in common upon the hind-quarters of a grunting pig snuffing for dross in Tothill fields.

Whenever there was a fresh supply of powder, this rusty fowling-piece would change hands, and the above pig was searched for, and a discharge of small shot propelled into its hams to try the range of the gun. At first the huge porker, so tickled up behind, would give a grunt, waggle its tail, run a few yards, and begin to snuff about as before; but at length, from long practice, its hinder extremities became more callous, and almost to be shot-proof, which obliged the juvenile marksmen to shorten the range to produce even a shake of the tail, or even a solitary grunt, so intent was the animal, like the rest of its species, on the more interesting process of enlarging its own belly and fattening its carcass, no doubt for such a knife as a man carries who was wont to swear visitors at Highgate.

Soon after nightfall, the 31st of December, 1814, our

convoy left the mouth of the Mississippi, and steered its course, in the Gulf of Florida, towards the entrance of Lac Borgne, or the blind lake near the Chandeleur islands.

On the morning of the 1st of January, 1815, a most exceedingly dense white fog hung upon the waters, and totally obscured all objects, and our convoy was obliged to lay too without knowing what position it had gained. Not a breath of wind agitated the waters, nor could one vessel see another even within half cable's length. All around about us we heard minute guns fired, as is customary in honour of some great funeral or doleful event. This extraordinary fog lasted for some hours, and eclipsed all objects; the most intense excitement was felt by us, intermingled with curiosity to discover, if possible, where we were and from whence came the long roll of the various cannon that were discharged as precautionary signals to hinder, if possible, one ship from running foul of the other. But here the imagination must be left to fill up the recital for some hours, figuring to itself how singularly impressive these intonations from the reports of the cannon must have sounded to our ears, having come so far, and then greeted by so singular an announcement that we were amidst invisible friends, or supposed to be so; for beyond the scope of a few planks on our own decks, the vision did not extend until late in the day. And what is not a little odd, during our long voyage, with the exception of the before mentioned piractical-looking vessel, and a distant man-of-war, that, since leaving England, I had hardly seen a strange sail, and while coasting along St. Domingo, Jamaica, and Cuba, not a single boat was seen by myself, or the canvass of any ship; and, while crossing the Gulf of Mexico, the usual vista of sky and water only added to the monotony of the scene.

After some hours suspense, the great fog by degrees cleared off, and we found ourselves encircled by a British fleet of at least sixty sail, including line of battle ships, frigates, sloops, transports, and other smaller craft lying at anchor. At the entrance of Lac Borgne the forlorn-looking coast or flats are covered with fir trees, and along the horizontal line, these trees in perspective appear to sink lower and lower, like the sable feathers upon a funeral hearse, until, they diminished as specks upon the water.

The greater part of the British fleet at anchor had come from the Chesapeake, after capturing Washington with the British on board, who malignantly set fire to some of its public buildings, which conflagration in a military or a civil point of view totally eclipsed all the honour and glory gained by a handful of British troops, while ascending the heights of Blandensburg. This act of incendiarism, instead of forwarding the interests of His Britannic Majesty had a contrary effect, and united the Americans as one man, to step forward boldly to save their homes from the torch of the incendiary. And would it be believed that these very troops, when they evacuated Washington, were under the necessity of leaving their badly wounded to the care of a people who had suffered from such dreadful destruction of property, and that these Americans would not soil their hands in the blood of the helpless, but on the contrary fostered these wounded soldiers who had fallen in the fair field of battle.

Soon after the capture of Washington, a similar attempt had been made by the same troops to endeavour to enter Baltimore, in front of which Major-General Ross was killed by an American marksman, when the second in command of the British troops retreated to his ships.

This fleet, being again reinforced with more ships and soldiers, run past the West Indies, to make an attempt on New Orleans. We cast anchor just within Lac Borgne, Here it will be necessary to notice, before taking farewell of the

Helen, which was afterwards loaded with stores on her passage to England, that she foundered at sea, and all hands perished, except a cabin boy, who, clinging to a hen-coop, was picked up by a vessel. He made known that the first mate of the *Helen* had accidentally blown his brains out, having put his foot upon the lock of a rusty musket while cleaning it, which exploded and put an end to him; and that the following day, the brig sunk so unexpectedly as not even to give the crew time to get out the long-boat; therefore the hole in the bottom was nothing imaginary, and, no doubt, much larger than was anticipated. This was the last of the *Helen*, her amiable master, well conducted mate, and crew. Most likely had she not floated as an ark, for myself and others across the Atlantic, her fate and that of her crew might have been consigned to the same oblivion of other craft, of small note and tonnage.

A thought now comes across my mind, that the officer whose company I succeeded to was, on the supposition of his being drowned, as he was never heard of after setting sail from the rock of Gibraltar, in a ship cargoed with rags, which was supposed to be seen on fire off the Spanish coast. This officer had also received a terrible gunshot wound in his breastbone, which, for a time was thought to be mortal; and what is more strange, that the captain, a fine young man, with whom I exchanged, when going on half-pay, was also drowned, on an excursion of amusement.

What my ultimate fate is to be, must be left in the inscrutable hands of Him above, who ordains all things for us vain worms, that crawl upon the earth for a span, flattering ourselves that we hand down to posterity the seasons, the winds, the waves, and less enduring pyramids, the hieroglyphics or the mummy.

Chapter 6

Towards New Orleans

The 3rd of January, men-of-war's boats came alongside, one sailor wore a bear's skin cap, like that represented on the head of Robinson Crusoe, others were unshaved and made unusually wild and shaggy configurations, after toiling so long in the boats unshaved. Each officer provided himself with a rolled cloak and blanket, to which was added a haversack, stuffed with a couple of shirts, two pairs of socks, a towel, a piece of soap, a tooth-brush, with an extra pair of shoes or boots. This being what is called light marching order, no other baggage being allowed ashore on this occasion.

Descending into one of these boats, we were soon stuffed, with two companies, into a small skiffer, usually employed in carrying cargoes of moist sugar from one West India island to another; the decks and the interior of the cabin were crusted with a sweet and sparkling substance, shining like sugar-candy, the cabin was so small that we could neither sit or lie down therein, and the half-decks were so crowded by the soldiers, that they could hardly move their limbs, but flattered themselves that a few hours would relieve them from their cramped and tedious positions. It was almost impracticable to move from one quarter of this small vessel to the other, without treading on hands, arms, legs, heads, and, indeed, on every part of the human frame, so closely packed were the crowd of living persons, many of whom attempted to climb up the scanty rigging, the ropes of which were likewise covered with the sweets of the sugar-cane, to endeavour for a brief space to stretch their stiffened and contracted limbs.

A midshipman commanded her, and during the murky hours of darkness was coiled up and shrouded by the Union Jack in the cabin, which was of such ridiculously small dimensions that a moderate-sized man could neither stand up nor lie down in it.

Aboard this skiffer an accident happened which was the very *né plus ultra* of all that could be most ridiculous; but as the occurrence might annoy the stranger whose lot it was to come among us, I must refrain from levity in detailing the accident which befell him and others farther than that His Majesty's Union Jack came in for a share of the good luck which plastered every individual in the cabin, its doorway, and its walls. The full-grown middy began to bluster with a strain of nautical phrases, but had no sooner jumped out of his place of refuge to show his authority than he was at once in the same doleful plight with the rest, and notwithstanding bravely exclaimed that he could have got over the mishap, but the idea of the Union Jack being so treated was abominable.

The following morning, in the Lac Borgne, we saw the five American schooners, or gunboats, which were moored in line about four hundred yards distant one from the other, which had been captured a few days before, the headmost was the last that surrendered, and carried a very heavy gun mounted upon a circular-traverse.

Although this lake is from fifteen to twenty miles in breadth in some parts, and about fifty miles in length, its waters are so shallow in many places that we got aground several times on oyster-beds, which almost rise to the surface of the water, and here and there above it; the shores on each side are perfectly flat, and principally covered with fir-trees.

After two days' pulling, hauling, and towing, on the 5th we reached, early at night, the mouth of a *creek,* twelve miles from New Orleans: we again shifted our berth, were hustled into launches and other row-boats, pulled by men-of-war's men. The country presents a perfect morass, and is covered with a sheet of reeds eight or nine feet high, with only one tree and a few miserable huts (not visible to us, owing to the darkness) to break the monotonous scenery for many miles. The water rises so near to the level of the bog that every ripple caused by the motion of a boat seemed as if it would overflow this dreary marsh, which is intersected with stagnant pools and narrow creeks of immense depth.

The sailors in the boat were amusing us with a description of the red men, who were now the allies of the British, and actually in their bivouac before New Orleans; and I must confess that my fancy was wrought up to the highest excitement to obtain a glimpse of these Indians, who, as stated, were in the habit of stealing through the reeds or underwood in these parts, for the purpose of discharging a rifle or a poisoned arrow at their enemies, who, dead or alive, was unmercifully scalped on the spot, the skin and the hair of the dead so torn off being one of their greatest and most esteemed trophies of distinction.

After two hours' rowing we saw a fire at a short distance to the left, this being the first signs of animation (to refer to Columbus) we had seen on shore in the New World. At the sight of this welcome beacon for landing our hearts bounded with inexpressible delight as we jumped on *terra firma,* or rather into a *morass,* covered with trampled reeds, which alone prevented our sinking into a clayey substance or quagmire. The only tent standing was compassed by scattered stores, such as barrels of salt junk and biscuits, rum-casks, sails, ropes, canoes, paddles, cannonballs, rammers, handspikes, ammunition, pitch-pots, and water-casks, which were piled together into a circle, in the middle of which a group of jolly tars had kindled a fire, whilst others were fast asleep, their heads stuck into casks or small barrels, which afforded them a little shelter from the night-dew after a hard day's pull.

The captain of the navy who superintended the debarkation of troops and stores at this spot invited us to his tent, and made us feel truly comfortable by a seasonable supply of hot grog, which was boiled in a cauldron. We then in merry mood started along the edge of the creek to join the army before New Orleans.

As we proceeded, the ground became by degrees firmer, and having passed through a small forest, at, midnight we joined the greater portion of our regiment, which had already landed from other boats. Here as many congratulations were exchanged between us as if we had been separated for years. The huts were constructed of sugar-canes; and rolled in our solitary blankets we slept as soundly during the night as if reposing on beds of down.

The following morning I saw, of men, women, and children, about two hundred Chickasaw and Choctaw Indians, who were squatting close on the left of our huts. Their outlandish-looking faces, like masks, deeply excited my attention and curiosity; the complexion of the men was a copper colour, and they were perfectly naked, with the exception of a girdle round their loins, with a dirty blanket or the skin of a wild beast slung round their necks, which hung down the back like a mantle. Nothing could exceed the hideousness of their countenances; the forehead projects in an extraordinary degree; the eyes are generally dark with a sullen expression; the eyebrows are broad and bushy; the nostrils are distended, from which hang a metal ring; the upper part of the bridge of the nose scarcely rises above the face, which is tattooed. Amongst some of them the two front teeth are pulled up, no doubt by little and little, to make them stick out horizontally; the teeth, so unnaturally placed, hold up the upper lip, which gives a truly savage aspect; their heads are large, with long black hair, the texture about as coarse as a horse's tail. In the afternoon they decorate themselves by rubbing their cheeks with a sort of red ochre, and intermingling with the hair the bright plumage of various birds, and when so adorned they sit cross-legged opposite a small fire, their eyes cast down as if in deep and important meditation, and in no instance, when thus bedizened, did I ever see them deign to give us a glance.

The married women, or squaws, are in a state of nudity, with the exception of one petticoat reaching to the middle of the calf of the leg; the daughters of twelve years of age are entirely without covering, and squat in the white ashes cross-legged, like their parents; and when they have occasion to move about, the ashes from the fire sticking like feathers to their posteriors, and as dame nature has cast the part in so many moulds, no further description can be requisite to assist the tittering faculties.

I did not see the three chiefs, or kings, in their real costume, as they were transmogrified and wore sergeants' jackets, the uniform of the staff-corps. Nothing could surpass their grotesque figures, assisted by the haughty, frowning, and important looks put on by them, which considerably added to their comic turnout.

One of these warrior-chiefs wore an old round hat (no doubt in compliment to the British) with a white feather stuck on one side, a red jacket, with broad skirts, like a shooting-jacket, and a pair of leather breeches open at the knees, without shoes or stockings, finished the *tout ensemble*. The other two kings wore the red jackets covered with a profusion of gold lace, but were *sans culottes* with a clout betwixt their naked copper-coloured legs.

If anything, they all turned the toe a little inwards, and raising the feet very high from the ground, as if walking amongst brambles or underwood, and then swing the knee, with a sort of flourish, they plant the foot firmly down, as if to imply that it had safely arrived without meeting with any tanglements or underwood in its descent, which usually intersect the forests of their encampments, where they no doubt acquire this style of walk from early life. The women, from carrying heavy loads, go along with a sort of springing jog trot; and the children, while running along, raising their little legs as if treading on hot embers, owing to the tenderness of their feet; this, imbibed from infancy, may account for the elders raising their feet as stated.

An officer was indiscreet enough to ask one of these chiefs to permit him to examine one of their scalping-knives; which was acceded to, accompanied by a look as black as thunder. We told the officer not to allow the chief to find out where his hut was placed, or to a certainty his wig would be ripped off his head before the morning.

When these chiefs dined with the general, one of them asked if the "King of England was as great a man as himself?" Indeed, nothing can surpass their pomposity. And as a general outline of these savages in a body, they resembled those figures descending the broad stairs at the Italian Opera house into the infernal regions in the ballet of *La Fauste*.

A few hundred yards behind our bivouac an immense brick warehouse was situated, from which enormous casks, filled with sugar, were rolled and converted into a battery. The proprietor's house was built of light materials, and standing on piles about the same height from the ground as the base of a hayrick, to protect it from being flooded when the Mississippi overflowed its artificial dyke. The river at this place is about eight hundred or a thousand yards in breadth, bringing in its rapid current huge forest-trees, many of which were still sticking in its muddy banks. Temporary sheds, constructed of wood, were clustered round the proprietor's house for the use of the black slaves which belong to this sugar-plantation; but where they found shelter during the floods I cannot say, but I suppose behind the thick and massive brick walls of the sugar-warehouse. Many of the negroes and negresses continued in these dwellings, but most of them had escaped to New Orleans, distant little more than five miles.

A half-moon detached battery, little more than a mile in front of this bivouac, was just in front of the right of the American lines on the high road, mounted with four pieces of cannon. Its exterior as well as the whole face of the flat country strongly reminded me of a similar battery that had been under my command in the marshes of Lincolnshire, in England, on the right bank of the river Humber, when I was little more than fifteen years of age.

In this bivouac before New Orleans I met my friend and former brother officer, Wilkinson, who was now a captain in the eighty-fifth light infantry, and acting as brigade-major to Major-General Gibbs. But, as was usual in service, on many occasions, he still wore the uniform of his regiment, consisting of a red jacket, with yellow facings, the shoulders set off with silver-bullion wings and plated scales, like the links of ancient armour.

An officer of the forty-third said, "Why, Wilky, how is it that you have not provided us with good quarters in New Orleans, as we expected?—Why, what the d——d have you been about?"

At this question Wilkinson looked exceedingly vexed;

and clapping his hand to his forehead, and colouring up deeply, he turned away, stamping his foot, according to his usual custom when put out, and giving his arm a peculiar swing, answered, "Oh! say no more about it." And then placing his arm within mine, we paced up and down for a long time, when he opened such a budget of astounding information, concerning the hesitation shown for the fourteen previous days, as to make the very military blood curdle in one's veins. And, on being further questioned, by myself, as to the great stoppage, answered, "Bullets stopped us—bullets—that's all!" but declared that the lines in front were now grown formidable, and that the only chance of taking them was by a well concerted and simultaneous rush, when, should the ditch prove too deep in front of these lines, short-planked ladders would be the only means to cross it, by raising them on end, and letting them drop across the ditch, and then for the assailants to run over them.

Wilkinson was one of the best military draughtsmen in the army, and all his maps and plans were executed in a correct manner, and highly finished.

Wilkinson was called the "little corporal," from his prompt and decided port while conveying refractory cadets to the black-hole for various misdemeanours committed at the Royal Military College, at Marlow, (now removed to Sandhurst.) The gallant end of this officer is not to be deplored as a soldier on the field of battle, so much as his after sufferings when mortally wounded.

Although the following statement may appear trivial and simple-minded to recount, still at intervals we relax and indulge in the rehearsal of those trifles that have afforded us amusement in days of yore. Besides, there is no good reason why these our pastimes should not be noticed in print, as, mayhap, some young persons may chance to peruse this book, who are fond of what is called light reading, the more so as youth and more advanced manhood are so nearly allied and identified with the phrase of *chacun à son gout.*

For instance, I once knew a worthy baronet, who was not, as we may say, very far advanced in life, who possessed much ready wit, was polite and exceedingly pleasant at his own table, and, withal, was once a cornet in the Lifeguards, as an additional recommendation. This baronet thought himself a great and experienced lapidary, and was passionately fond of varnishing flint stones, and making, as he thought, a collection of thunderbolts, which were brought to him by those peasantry that knew his hobby, by whole barrow-loads, for the lapidary to pick and choose from the lot. The baronet, thinking that I was patience personified, one day, after dinner, conducted me into his *sanctum sanctorum*, and, with a transport of delight, pointed to one corner of the room, which was piled up with varnished flints of all shapes and sizes, with a second pile not quite so large, of his imaginary thunderbolts, after a long lecture, and expatiating on the beauty and the variety of his collection.

As an especial mark of favour he presented me with three flints and two thunderbolts. When descending into the drawing-room, would it be believed that I found myself envied in possession of these stores, and some little jealousy was exhibited by some of the lapidary's older but less favoured friends. Making my bow at my departure, I was much joked about these flints and thunderbolts, weighing some pounds, within the coils of my bandana handkerchief; and thus loaded I afforded considerable amusement to my companion in the vehicle, who every now and then looked, as he said, to see whether the horse in the gig was about to knock up with such a load at his hoofs.

After I had returned from the Walcheren expedition to England, Wilkinson was appointed as lieutenant in the same corps to which I belonged, and we soon became intimate friends, and for months were busily employed with the chisel and the penknife in shaping a small baronial castle of wood, which was flanked with loop-holed and embattled towers. The gate between the round towers was also protected by a portcullis, and over the space within the walls from the keep, a drawbridge was thrown over; the links of the chain that supported it were formed of sheet tin, which was cut into strips with a strong pair of scissors, and then rolled into links. Painted glass windows were inserted in the gothic apertures of the keep, and a little gilded silken flag was placed on its summit.

We also cut out about one hundred and fifty little wooden soldiers, and painted them. The officers being ornamented with gold and silver paper, according to their respective ranks, and all being completed, this castle was besieged, not with a battering-ram, but with small brass cannon, of a calibre which carried swan shot. Before a breach was practicable, all the staff and superior officers were put *hors de combat,* when a sergeant, who defended a round tower, was promoted to the rank of colonel and lieutenant-governor; and, after a warm wrangle between Wilkinson and myself, at his skipping over the grades of ensign, lieutenant, captain, and major, it was finally arranged that none under the rank of colonel could have the honour of taking charge of the castle. The *ci-devant* sergeant being armed with a tin sword, was repainted and covered with a profusion of silver paper, cutting a most dashing and brilliant appearance, and having risen to this rank from the working soldier, it was determined to give him a benefit of the post of honour, that is to say, the hottest berth in the castle. The siege went on, many fell by his side, but the *ci-devant* sergeant seemed endowed with a charmed exterior.

Richards, the paymaster of our regiment, was most exceedingly annoyed at the many and loud reports of the cannon at this long siege, which took place in the next room to his apartments; but, at length, was so excited that he would throw down his pen to see how things were going on; and seeing the almost supernatural escapes of the lieutenant-governor, with sterling warmth, he entreated that the fire of the brass cannon should be directed to another quarter of the castle without effect; and when the paymaster heard that the *ci-devant* sergeant had at last fallen, he burst out of the room in a fit of despair at the unfair way that he had been treated.

For days afterwards he would enter the room, and say, "really I cannot forget that poor sergeant;" and protesting that such was the force of custom from the reports of the little cannon day after day, he failed to cast up his accounts with half the correctness since the noise had ceased.

Years afterwards, having some of those little figures in a small case, whilst disembarking in England from France, a custom-house officer looked at them; when I told him that I had made them; "Oh, poh, poh!" replied he, "they are of French manufacture; but I shall not notice trifles like these."

Some of these little figures I possess to the present day.

CHAPTER 7

Hallen's Defence

Having proceeded so far, regarding our own immediate movements and adventures, it may be as well, as a key to the whole of the transactions which took place before our arrival off the coast, to state briefly such circumstances as were related, on the spot, to myself by those whose veracity may be depended on.

And here I must premise, by saying that I have invariably found in the bivouac or the tented field undisguised truths laid bare, either regarding a surprise, a victory, or a defeat, and the minutiae of all occurrences detailed with unvarnished tale.

The broad and wholesome language which is held over the flaring-up or the dying embers of the camp-fires, is a good telegraphic lesson for men of the world. Here the utmost good-nature prevails. A spirit of emulation undoubtedly exists, and certain corps stand high, and are acknowledged pre-eminent according to their several practical merits, and are looked up to with an unjaundiced eye. And this I dwell on, because he who writes must make up his mind to go straight ahead, and to strain every nerve to wrestle and to endeavour to disentangle himself from the stumbling blocks and the literary cords which are too often in ready coils to shackle the pen, and to hoodwink him, who offers his genuine mite to the stock of unmutilated history.

But, in after times, when past events are disinterred and brought to light, they are too often ill-digested, and engender rancour in the breasts of those craving praise on hot-pressed paper, for that which they could not grapple with or execute in the face of an enemy. Victory elicits praise, defeat seldom; except, perchance, by some of those who can only boast of figuring in what is called a "fine retreat."

Now it will be absolutely necessary to portray, for the elucidation of the reader, how it came to pass that we found the British force at the spot of ground which they had possessed themselves of at midday, the previous 23rd of December, 1814; and seven days before our arrival off the immense flats of West Florida.

However, to cut the matter short, New Orleans, the capital of Louisiana, counted at this time a mixed population of twenty thousand souls, coming from the parent stock of Spaniards, French, Creoles, Americans, negro slaves, and coffin-makers. The warehouses of the city were amply stored with cotton to a vast amount, and also sugar, molasses, tobacco, and other products of this prolific soil, which, at flood water-mark of the Mississippi, is only protected by the *levée de terre,* or bank, from a submersion of those united waters, running more than three thousand seven hundred miles from the interior, through vast solitudes of forests and prairies, which, like a great artery, is at times boiling over with the countless watery veins from the embrochures of the great American continent.

The ground around about, and on which New Orleans is built, is called the "Wet Grave," owing to the ravages caused by the yellow fever amongst its mixed population for the space of eight months in the year.

In this part of the country the water springs up a foot or

two from the surface of the earth, so that the coffins of the dead have a weight attached to them, or are sunk by pressure to the bottom of the watery grave. The more affluent orders of society build vaults, as in other countries; by this means forming a dry resting place for a time, for the bodies of the defunct.

The city is one hundred miles inland from the mouth of the Mississippi, and situated immediately on its left bank, and is otherwise enclosed by a vast wilderness of swamps, lakes, creeks, and mucky impassable forests, through which the city is only approachable by a few roads or causeways, and the narrow passage of the Mississippi is protected by the guns of fort Saint Philippe, which is built upon piles.

The whole extent of these regions is composed of one dead flat, save here and there an artificial bank, or *levée de terre*, which protects the soil from being undermined by the waters of the river and melted into a morass, which, during some of the floods, as well as the city of New Orleans itself, might some day, with its living and dead, be carried by piecemeal into the Gulf of Florida.

This city of the swamps is visited from time to time by the forlorn and sallow-faced squatters, the bear-hunters and the backwoodsmen coming down the river as they do from their remote settlements or log-houses, which are merely constructed with a few trunks of trees; and some of these log-houses are situated in such marshy places, that it is necessary for the squatter to have the rough outlines of a boat ready at hand to place his chattels therein in case of a sudden inundation.

In these arks or boats,* these men descend the Missis-

---

* The steam-boats now plying on the Mississippi must change the aspect of the river, and the backwoodsmen can ascend the current quicker than they come down it. This wonderful change in a few years will be of incalculable benefit for trading with the interior.

sippi in a few days to New Orleans, where the arks are sold or bartered away, to be used as fire-wood, coffins, or for other domestic purposes. Thus disposed of, whole months are consumed by these pilgrims in exploring their way, whence they came, either knee-deep and wading through marshes, or paddling in a light canoe, or drawing a boat with ropes against the current of the river to the hut of their seclusion, which is generally far removed from society or the haunts of man.

And, although ten or twelve days might have brought them down the river, yet its navigation is so beset with difficulties as to require months travel or voyage to regain that quarter of the globe which individually they may have emerged from.

Therefore, to speak technically, the "Wet Grave" at this time was only approachable by him wielding a hostile sword, either poised through the air, assisted by the aerial flight of the bird of prey, or astride of the alligator's scaly back, to enable him to get through such a slough.

Notwithstanding all these natural drawbacks, the city of New Orleans, with its valuable booty of merchandise, was craved for by the British to grasp such a prize by a *coup de main*. But information having reached that place through the master of a trading vessel from Jamaica, who there had heard that such an attempt was in agitation, the American government sent Andrew Jackson, Esq. to look out for the British, and to defend New Orleans.

The British fleet was commanded by Admiral Sir Alexander Cochrane, who, having crossed the Gulf of Mexico, cast anchor off the Chandeleur Islands on the 8th of December, 1814, near the mouth of Lac Borgne, where Rear-Admiral Malcolm joined on the 11th, three days after, with his reinforcement to the fleet.

The land-force, including two regiments of blacks, on

board the fleet, under the orders of Major-General Sir John Treane, including officers, consisted of four thousand seven hundred soldiers, amongst whom were a squadron of the fourteenth light dragoons, with their saddles and bridles, and other cavalry gear, ready to place upon the backs of American horses, so soon as they should be fortunate enough to obtain them.

The anchorage of the British fleet was sixty-six or seventy miles from New Orleans by the way of Lac Borgne.

The British commanders, finding that their intended *coup de main* was anticipated by the Americans, and that the ways, or causeways, to New Orleans were barricaded and defended by troops, cannon, and other impediments, it was resolved, in the true spirit of enterprise, to enter Lac Borgne, notwithstanding the shoals and shallows by which its navigation was intersected; this being the only chance still left open to approach the city of the swamps. And should the attempt succeed to obtain a firm footing, the troops were then to use their arms and bayonets according to circumstances, and from the known character of the Americans, there being little doubt that blood would flow. The sooner the British could bring the few regular troops, and the *posse comitates* of the Americans to trial, the greater was their chance of ultimate success. As this mode of attack was still grounded upon a sort of *coup de main,* and possibly to bring the Americans to battle at fault.

This enterprise, executed in winter time, of short days, and long nights, and *malgré* baffling winds, intense cold, shoals, a difficult navigation, and its attendant accompaniments, a more daring thought could not have been devised. And, as far as the marine exertions went, there was no lack of skill or assistance withheld in putting it into execution.

The 12th of December, the pinnaces, launches, and barges of the squadron were placed under the orders of

Captain Lockyer, R. N. commander of the sloop *Sophie*, with orders to go into Lac Borgne in search of some vessels that had run into the lake to join others already there for its defence. The man-of-wars' boats were formed into three divisions—one under Captain Montresor of the *Manly*, and the other under Captain Roberts of the *Meteor*.

Before daylight, on the morning of the 13th, the boats, armed with carronades, entered the lake, and, after a pull of thirty-six hours, against the wind and strong currents, the boats came, on the morning of the 14th, within sight of five American gun-vessels, which were moored off Saint Joseph's Island, the shallows preventing their running further up the lake. And Captain Roberts having previously taken an armed sloop that had attempted to join the American gunboats, which were drawn out in line, the broadsides of this flotilla facing the advance of the British, ready to give battle.

The boats, having got into more dense order, threw out their grapplings, to get some refreshment, within a short pull of the enemy's line.

All being ready, the signal was given to advance, and when the boats were in good range the Americans pounded away; the boats' crews cried "Give way!" and cheered loudly; hence it became a boat-race, and the Americans being moored in line, at least four hundred yards apart one from the other, the attacking boats were a good deal divided, and each boat pulling away wildly came to close quarters.

The clouds of smoke rolled upwards, and the splashing of round and grape shot in the water, and the loud exhortations of "Give way!" presented an animated scene at midday. Captain Lockyer, in the barge of the *Seahorse*, was first up to the mark, and his boat's crew was most uncourteously handled by the American commodore, who at first would not let Captain Lockyer get aboard, and a rough tussle took place; but other boats coming up, the sailors, sword in hand, being covered by the fire from the small arms of the marines, cut away their defensive netting that was coiled round her decks like a spider's web. The British at last mastered the Americans, and captured all the five vessels in succession, making their different crews prisoners, but not before some of the guns of the captured vessels had been turned upon those that still resisted, to enable the boarders to complete their victory. The headmost vessel was the last that gave in, and Jack-tar was fain to brush aside his locks and turn a quid before she struck the colours of the Union.

Captain Lockyer was wounded, and including naval and marine officers, sailors, and private marines, the loss was severe, amounting, amongst the different boats' crews, to ninety-four killed and wounded; and indeed the sailors pulling up with their heavy oars is a serious job, the balls knocking off their heads and piercing from behind is quite enough to excite the sculler now and then to cast a hasty glance over either shoulder to see what is coming next.

The blue jackets and the red (marines) had now cleared the lake for the passage of the troops, and their exertions were well worthy of the old signal at Trafalgar.

On the 16th the advance, under Colonel Thornton and Captain Sir James Gordon of the *Seahorse* frigate, were put into boats, and took post upon the Isle aux Poix, a small swampy spot at the mouth of the Pearl River, distant thirty miles from the anchorage and twenty miles from the head of the Bayou Catalan, up which it was intended to proceed towards New Orleans. Major-General Keane, Admiral T. A. Cochrane, and Admiral Sir R. Codrington followed on the 17th, and took post with the troops on the Isle aux Poix.

An officer of the marines was sent to the Choctaws, a tribe of Indian savages assembled on the main, to negotiate with them for their cooperation with the British. Two officers were also sent with a guide towards the entrance of the Bayou Catalan, and these officers proceeded in a canoe up a creek, the head of which suddenly ceases to flow within five miles and a half of New Orleans. These officers, without interruption, returned from their critical enterprise to the headquarters, to report the important tidings that there was not yet any opposition shown at this point to prevent a landing.

By the 21st all the land forces were concentrated upon the Isle au Poix, situated about equidistant from the anchorage of the fleet and the destined place of landing. The boats having experienced rough and severe weather of rain and frost, the sailors were a good deal harassed by their almost supernatural exertions in putting on shore the troops at the Isle aux Poix, in readiness to support those who were to push towards New Orleans in advance.

The morning of the 22nd, at ten o'clock, a.m., General Keane embarked from the Isle aux Poix in gun-vessels, boats, and other craft, with a force of two thousand four hundred soldiers, one thousand six hundred being told off in the lightest boats as a vanguard, and before they had sailed three miles one of the largest vessels grounded, and many of the other craft every now and then came as hard and fast on the shoals as if at anchor. Notwithstanding this extraordinary water scene of vessels and boats scattered far and wide, and although night was coming on, nothing daunted, General Keane and Admiral Malcolm pushed on with the advanced guard, and after dark they reached the mouth of the Bayou or Creak Catalan, which communicates with lakes Borgne and Ponchartrain.

Captain Traverses company of riflemen were pulled ahead, and seeing a fire on the right-hand side of the creek, and a short way within its mouth, these riflemen quietly stepped ashore, and making a simultaneous rush they contrived to capture the whole of this lookout American picket without a single gun of alarm having been discharged by either party.

This spot is called Des Pêcheurs, or the fishermen's huts, about sixteen miles from New Orleans. These huts are constructed upon an artificial mound, which is enclosed by a vast swamp, covered by reeds growing ten or twelve feet in height, and tapering to a point. The stem of this reed is very strong, and in colour resembling a bamboo cane.

The taking of the American picket was indeed the happy harbinger, and one of the mainsprings on which final success might be reckoned, and the spirits of the vanguard were raised accordingly.

The straggling boats then dashed up the creek, which is enclosed on either side by a vast sea of reeds. Soon after daylight, a few of the troops made good their landing on the left-hand side of the creek, within seven miles of New Orleans during the previous night, the other boats coming up one by one. What a water scene was here, boats aground or straggling nearly all the way to the Isle aux Poix, a distance of thirty miles. The sailors had been in their boats for eight days and nights, and some of the soldiers had likewise been six days and nights, either on a chilly desolate island or in boats.

Early in the day of the 23rd* one thousand six hundred British troops were landed within seven miles of New Or-

---

* At the city of Ghent, in Flanders, the English and the American commissioners were negotiating off and on, to adjust the differences between Great Britain and the Union, from August, 1814, until the following 24th of December of the same year. The preliminaries of peace were settled at Ghent, consisting of eleven articles, on the very day after the British force had made good their landing in the immediate neighbourhood of New Orleans. Peace between His Britannic Majesty and the United States of America was finally ratified at Washington the 17th of February, 1815.

leans, and marching through a small wood they came upon more solid ground near the head of the Bayou, and reached a house and plantation near the bank of the Mississippi, where the same company of riflemen, which had taken the American picket the night before, now again took a major and twenty armed American militia-men, in coloured clothes, prisoners, within six miles of New Orleans, without a shot being discharged on either side, or an individual left at liberty to carry any intelligence of so wonderful an arrival of armed visitors so near the city. Unfortunately the captive major effected his escape, and conveyed the news of the landing of the British to Orleans. This dashing enterprise almost rivalled, upon a small scale, the far-famed march of Bonaparte across the Alps, so renowned in history.

Up to this moment the gun-vessels taken, the Americans kidnapped at the mouth of the creek, and the domesticated militia-men swept off and made prisoners around the house of a Monsieur Vilette, and all without a gun being exploded to stop the spring tide of good fortune attending the invaders' career, so honourable, so adventurous, and so well deserving a meed of praise. There had been no real link of communication between the American flotilla and their lookout posts, and they were so far separated that one body was totally unconnected with the other; added to which there was no effective lookout even at the head of the creek, which all at once ceased to flow near this spot like the top of an extinguisher, and along the bank within a mile or two of its head, being the only contracted place or loop-hole where a hostile force could land, and where a handful of Americana from behind the trees might have annihilated those in the boats, as they straggled up the creek one after the other.

The British troops now penetrated an unsightly marsh, whose pools and deep creeks were canopied over with the putrid exhalations from the swamps; and these desolate regions were without doubt the rendezvous of the universe for wild ducks, and the resort of hideous and floundering alligators that pop their heads up and down as plentiful as bullfrogs in some stagnant pools.

These swamps, now chilly and cold, in summer time present a different aspect, the temperature being as hot as an oven, and generating myriads of large mosquitoes, which pierce the legs with their stings, even through a pair of Russia-duck trousers.

All the difficulties were now over, and a flat open plain, with a swampy cypress and pine-wood was on the right hand, and the Mississippi river, twice as broad as the Thames at Westminster Bridge, on the left, and the open city of New Orleans five miles and a half in front, where the American citizens and their helps were peaceably and unconsciously serving behind their counters, in their stores or shops: there was not a single obstacle worthy of naming to stop the march of the soldiers.

And here did one thousand six hundred British troops halt, with their knapsacks on, their arms in their hands, at midday the 23rd of December, within sight of an insignificant skeleton, or rather the outline of a sham crescent battery, thrown up by the side of the high road to New Orleans, which was said to possess two pieces of cannon; a common ditch, such as is often seen in low grounds, extended one thousand yards from behind the outlines of this battery to the swampy wood as described, which might have been forded or crossed with planks, as an abundance of such materials was at hand, even supposing the gunners of these two pieces of cannon were invincible. But it never has been proved that these gunners were even at the battery ready to serve these guns—that there was a ball or a round of ammunition, or even a handspike at the battery at the time in question.

But this is a subject unworthy to descant or to dwell upon; for putting aside the great service that these two pieces of cannon would have been in the hands of the British, had they been at once taken possession of; fortune is a female, as military and other writers attest; neglect her today and she vanishes tomorrow. The hand of fortune beckoned the ruddy strangers from the old country to embrace a prize, and such a prize as is seldom offered *gratis* in war. But the soldiers of Washington were now of marble temperature, and almost as immovable as the Egyptian pyramids. Speaking historically, with outstretched arms did the slighted maid of Orleans, with blind and even neglected zeal, often turn the balance in favour of the strangers. But, alas!, the maid might as well have implored the tide to cease to flow as to move the British troops, who now acted as if they were metamorphosed into fixtures, or were bound by some magic spell.

Therefore, up to this never-to-be-obliterated crisis, Andrew Jackson, Esquire, was virtually surprised, and the city of New Orleans, with its rich merchandise, and its flock, speaking many tongues, which had been consigned to his protection, was within an ace of encountering a much more inglorious fate than Washington, the seat of Congress and the heart's core of the Union, had met with a few months before by some of the same British troops now standing hood-winked at the open portals of New Orleans.

By this it would appear that the *fair fame* of Andrew Jackson, Esquire, was not hanging on a thread, or on the turn of a straw, but rested merely on the caprice and pleasure of the British general. There was still five hours' light; but the whole day was lost, and the troops halted at the very time they ought to have gone on. Two American vessels were seen anchored up the river, but no notice was taken of them, or rather no preparations were made to receive them should they slip their cables, although the spot which the British were now holding was a contracted space of ground within a few hundred yards of the Mississippi. One staff officer advised that time should be taken by the forelock; that the British troops should make an instantaneous advance; but his voice was nought in the balance of the military scale, and his supposed hasty opinions were overruled by his seniors.

In the afternoon a few armed American horsemen came up the main road from New Orleans, which runs parallel with the river, to take a peep at a company of English riflemen who were pushed out from the main body as a picket, and who had taken almost as many American prisoners as its own original numbers. This picket was relieved by Captain Hallen's company. A few shots were discharged by the riflemen at the American horsemen, who were dressed in coloured clothes, wearing broad beavers, and armed with long duck guns, rifles, or any other weapons of defence first coming to hand.

After this reconnaissance they wheeled about and took post behind the outlines of the aforesaid crescent battery. But Andrew Jackson, Esquire, having had a respite, briefly gathered his men into some order; and knowing that Orleans, the present scene of tumult, was no place to fight, in fact no place of defence, now seized as it were a sledgehammer, and after the manner of grasping a truncheon, invoked Mars to waive military forms or etiquette, and at once resolved to figure as a *war general*.

Night was now coming on apace; and the British troops already landed consisted of the fourth regiment, or King's own, the eighty-fifth light infantry regiment, and five companies of the ninety-fifth, or rifles, with two light three-pounders, and a few military artificers. These soldiers were lounging about; and as the boats had returned to extricate

67

those left aground in the lake and those already landed having no retreat, it might have been conjectured that, like one of Caesar's legions of old, they would have felled trees, or made some strong hold in case of exigencies, as a *point d'appui*, as they were determined to halt. But no such thing was done, although, as before stated, an impassable morass lay behind them.

Fires now blazed in the bivouac and all around Monsieur Villerey's house, and many lights showed the dark outlines of men passing to and fro, and busily employed cooking in the kettles belonging to the slaves of the plantation—the surrounding adjacents being shrouded and overcast with the gloom of night. Some of the soldiers were asleep, whilst others were partaking of a warm meal after a long fast. In this happy state of security his Britannic majesty's troops were indulging, their arms piled, and each soldier looking after his little immediate necessities.

Their vanguards were in front at the usual military distance; when, at eight o'clock, a heavy splash in the river was distinctly heard by some of the troops. This soon proved to be the American sloop which had been seen up the river, of fourteen guns; and after dark coming down, now let go her anchor, and swinging round her head to the current, with her broadside facing, within a few hundred yards of the bivouac, where the fires, like so many land-marks or beacons enabled the Americans to point their guns accordingly. But the sloop being shrouded by the robe of night, the carousers ashore were quite ignorant and heedless of the heavy splash in the water. All being prepared on board the sloop, and *vice versa* all being unprepared on shore, a sonorous voice was heard to exclaim, in broad English, as if rising out of the waters of the Mississippi, "Now, d—n their eyes, give it 'em!" And as the flashes from the cannon reflected for a moment the outlines of the ominous sloop on the water, so plunged the round and grape-shot like so many thunder-bolts amongst the astounded troops, the balls boring down whole piles of arms, knocking kettles off the fires, scattering blazing beams of wood about, maiming some soldiers, and sending others whence no traveller returns.

This was enough to put one of Caesar's legions in a panic; and, if from such an astounding fact, the troops had even retired, could it be wondered at? But no; they were veterans and brave troops; and, probably, a more trying situation seldom happens. The *levée de terre,* or bank of the river, being only three feet above the level of the water, was no screen in the first instance; and thus, round after round, and ball after ball, were vomited forth, driving the troops into most dire confusion, which caused a tenfold panic during the darkness, and the confusion beggars all description; no mob could be in a more utter state of disorganization.

Some took shelter under the bank of the river, behind the house, or any other place of refuge nearest at hand, to screen themselves from the ferocious visitation. Officers were buckling on their swords, and throwing down knives and forks, and calling on their soldiers. Soldiers were look-ing after their arms or buckling on their knapsacks, and calling to their officers. Bugle-horns were sounding, while the soldiers were striving to gather together, or to make some sort of formation; and all the time under the fire of this floating battery at point-blank range, and without any effective aim to silence these seven noisy monsters, the fire of which was assisted, when some of the fires were extin-guished, by the confusion of voices amongst the soldiers.

The balls of the American sloop thus made the British headquarters the most dangerous post, being, indeed, a most rare occurrence to happen; and had it not been for the very acceptable bank of the river, and other adjacents, affording opaque screens, or a rallying point for the disjointed troops from the murderous projectiles falling all around them, the consequences might have been more serious.

This novel way of assembling, or rather of scattering, the organized bands of discipline, and veterans to boot, was a war innovation, which effectively did away with the old system of the beating of drums, or the bugle horns sounding *"Turn out the whole,"* as practiced on sudden cases of emergency. And can it be wondered at that this floating battery of heavy calibre, like an assassin, shrouded in darkness, or whose form is concealed in the ample folds of a mantle, and putting us in mind of the Venetian bravo, with his cloak, sword, and lantern, ever and anon, as he thrusts, cuts, and maims, with his two-edged rapier with one hand, while he puts forth or withdraws the other, while grasping a lantern, whose bright rays dazzle and confound the footsteps of the benighted individual who may be groping his way through crooked monastic streets, when the rest of animation have sunk into sleepy oblivion—can it be wondered at, then, that such a coarse salutation caused such great confusion and outcry amongst the soldiers, and to use a homely phrase, put *the headquarters orderly room in a great tumult?*

Captain Hallen's company of riflemen were up and ready, and standing to their arms in proud array at the vanguard on the high road, the river protecting their left flank, and burning for a trial of strength with the long vaunted prowess of the American riflemen; and were resolved to see whether the Americans could beat a small part of the former "light division," even with their own boasted weapon, the rifle.

A company of the eighty-fifth light infantry were also stationed on picket at a house and garden in echelon to the right, and rather in rear of Hallen's picket; and hearing the raging tumult in their own rear, with the continued roar of cannon almost in the same direction, they unfortunately took an erroneous view of passing events, and evacuated this important post before they had fired a single round at the Americans, who quietly ensconced themselves in this house and garden, which, until it was afterwards retaken by the eighty-fifth regiment, and a portion of the rifle-corps, formed a rallying and important post for the enemy, who threw out irregular bodies to annoy the British during the after action.

Now, had Hallen, with his riflemen, done the same, and given up his post on the naked high road, although his position, taken in a military point of view, was no longer safe, the result might have proved most deplorable, at a moment too when the alarm-post at headquarters was utterly disorganized, and required a little breathing time to prepare for defensive or offensive operations.

When the great tumult at headquarters was at its height, a few shots were exchanged in front of Hallen's vanguard. This was General Jackson coming in person with three thousand regular troops and militiamen to the fight, the latter in coloured clothes. Some even assert that they counted more men than here specified. Captain Hallen began the battle on the high road singlehanded, against part of the seventh and forty-fourth American regiments, who were followed up by a strong body of irregulars.

But will posterity believe it, that all their most desperate attacks failed to beat Hallen's eighty men. They fought foot to foot and hand to hand, and, probably, since the invention of gunpowder, there is no instance on record of two opposing parties fighting so long muzzle to muzzle. Here, round after round, and volley after volley were exchanged. But although this picket was unsupported, the Americans could not gain the vital object, that of forcing the main road. The other pickets having retired from Hallen's right, left his company and its detachment isolated, like a ball of fire, to fight for themselves.

Owing to this, the lumps and crowds of American militia, who were armed with rifles, and long hunting knives for close quarters, now crossed the country; and by degrees getting nearer to the headquarters of the British, they were met by some companies of the rifle-corps and the eighty-fifth light infantry; and here again such confusion took place as seldom occurs in war—the bayonet of the British and the knife of the American were in active opposition at close quarters during this eventful night, and, as pronounced by the Americans, it was "rough and tumble."

The darkness was partially dispelled for a few moments, now and then, by the flashes of firearms; and whenever the outlines of men were distinguishable, the Americans called out "don't fire, we are your friends!" prisoners were taken and retaken. The Americans were litigating and wrangling, and protesting that they were not taken fairly, and were hugging their firearms and bewailing their separation from a favourite rifle that they wished to retain as their lawful property.

The British soldiers likewise, hearing their mother-tongue spoken, were captured by this deception; when such mistakes being detected, the nearest American received a knock-down blow; and in this manner prisoners on both sides having escaped, again joined in the fray, calling out lustily for their respective friends. Here was fighting, and straggling flashes of fire darting through the gloom, like the tails of so many comets.

At this most remarkable night-encounter the British were fighting on two sides of a ragged triangle, their left face pounded by the fire from the sloop, and their right face engaged with the American land-force. Hallen was still fighting in front at the apex.

At one time the Americans pushed round Hallen's right, and got possession of the high road behind him, where they took Major Mitchell and thirty riflemen going to his assistance. But Hallen was inexorable, and at no time had more than one hundred men at his disposal; the riflemen coming up from the rear by twos and threes to his assistance, when he had lost nearly half his picket in killed and wounded. And behind him was such confusion that an English artillery officer declared that the flying illumination encircling him was so unaccountably strange that had he not pointed big brass cannon to the front at the beginning of the fight, he could not have told which was the proper front of battle, as the English soldiers were often firing one upon the other, as well as the Americans, except by looking towards the muzzle of his three-pounder, which he dared not fire, from the fear of bringing down friends and foes by the same discharge; seeing, as he did, the darkness suddenly illuminated across the country by the flashing of muskets at every point of the compass.

At last, after three hours struggling, the Americans gave way, finding that the main body of their force could not gain possession of the high road; for the defence of which Hallen, who was badly wounded, and his brave company deserve great applause, being the only troops engaged, that steadily maintained their original front throughout the night.

All this scrambling contest fell principally upon the five companies of the green rifle-corps, composed of four hundred men, and the eighty-fifth regiment of light infantry, in all about one thousand strong. These fifteen companies lost in killed, wounded, and prisoners, two hundred and twenty-seven men out of the gross loss of this night, which was two hundred and forty-eight men.

The fourth regiment, or king's own, were in reserve, and only suffered a trifling loss; and one hundred and thirty of the ninety-third highlanders, and four companies of the twenty-first, or Royal North British Fusiliers, came up from the boats at the close of the fight, and proved a seasonable reserve at that crisis, this additional force swelling the British force to two thousand men, by merely deducting the already named loss, so that, at the end of the night's combat, the British mustered one hundred and fifty effective men more on the ground than when they began the action.

Neither ancient nor modern history can show a parallel resistance made against General Jackson by Captain Hallen and his company, and all the honour and glory is due to him and his lieutenants and soldiers for this heroic defence with such small means, and so much exposed as they were against such superior odds, at a time too when the main body of the British were nothing more or less than a confused mob in uniform, and coming forward to engage the Americans by twenties and thirties, or smaller numbers, as they could be scraped together, to be ready to engage, the eighty-fifth and the rifles being mixed together in one mass of confusion, and at one spot they formed behind some thin palings, the Americans on the other, engaged them muzzle to muzzle, every bullet piercing these frail defences, which only served as a shallow screen to separate friends and foes, who called to one another in English, and on more than one occasion, two enemies with loaded pieces were obliged to hold a parley in the dark before either of them could venture to pull a trigger in the other's face.

Here was, indeed, the old Shorncliffe style of challenging of "advance one, and give an account of yourself;" as an old soldier once questioned an officer, whom he well knew, by demanding "who served the regiment with pipe-clay?"

However, this singular night-combat finished by the Americans sustaining a galling loss in killed, wounded, and some prisoners; and after three hours' firing, hallooing, and shouting, within about the space of a square mile, they were thoroughly routed, and the little order they possessed when first coming on was totally evaporated, and now in turn they were in the most deplorable state of disorganization, a perfect rabble, and flying in all directions, and here and there groups were encumbered with their numerous wounded, perfect strangers as many of these Americans were one to the other, who were now scattered over the fields which were here and there intersected with drains and ditches for the irrigation of different plantations.

And, however droll it may seem to recount, General Jackson, as a last resource, laid hold of some of his *posse comitatus* that were wandering about in utter darkness, and implored them to sit down one by one, in a row along the edge of the aforesaid ditch, ten feet wide, where most probably not an American would have stopped, if their sinking courage had not been upheld by the flashes and the reports from the guns of the sloop which played throughout the night into the bivouac of the British. The Americans were in such utter route, that straggling persons extended to the very portals of New Orleans.

CHAPTER 8

Preparing for Attack & Defence

The British having won the victory had no more to do than to follow it up, at latest the next morning at daylight, when they would have found more real security under the windows of New Orleans than allowing themselves to be tamely besieged (an odd term to use of troops in an open bivouac) at a time when they might have acted on the offensive with so much less danger to themselves than continuing in their exposed position.

However, the morning of the 24th broke sluggishly, and the smoking ports of the sloop (it was a sore thorn in the side of the British headquarters) still projected its iron thunder amongst the besieged—for how can persons be designated otherwise under such circumstances? The British troops would have been too glad to have been ordered to advance from a spot where they were so annoyed. And, by marching on the skirts of the wood on their right, they might have reached New Orleans free from harm of any consideration at the distance of a mile from the American sloop and the ship of sixteen guns, and also nearly three quarters of a mile from the crescent battery, which being isolated, and once turned, would have been no longer tenable.

As a proof thereof, this field-work, which was open from

behind, in the end swelled into importance, as a sort of memento of the utter want of enterprise on the part of the British general. And in front of this battery hinged a series of military manoeuvres more remarkable than perhaps is to be shown in the annals of the world. And, alas, it proved too true that insignificant objects are not to be despised, and left to be captured at the will and pleasure of the dilatory.

The whole of this day was lost by the British general and thereby gained by his opponent, the former preferring to keep his troops under an irritating fire rather than move on. Every five minutes gained by the Americans was of vital importance, and every hour lost by the British who were waiting for reinforcements was the coming death-blow to their final hopes of success; for fresh troops and guns were in like manner coming from a distance to the assistance of General Jackson, and the hopes of the Americans were excited, supposing the British were really crippled, which was not the case. The whole of this day most of the people now placed under martial law in New Orleans were anxiously looking for the entrance of the British, minute after minute, and were lost in chagrin and amazement when night again closed without their entrance into the city.

By the morning of the 25th all the scattered remains of the British force were landed by piecemeal, hour after hour, from the Isle aux Poix, owing to the prodigious exertions of the sailors. All eyes were still cast on the American schooner, whose sides still smoked by day, and at night vomited iron harbingers from its ports into the bivouac of the British, so that, in point of fact, the city of New Orleans and General Jackson now became only a secondary consideration, and the discussion was how to get rid of this watery dragon; for the destruction of which heavy guns were sent for to the fleet, if possible, to blow her out of the water.

General Jackson profiting by this floating deception, placed there to allure the British general, took advantage of his own manoeuvre, which fortunately for him had the desired effect; and he prolonged the broad ditch by making a cut across the high road to the bank of the Mississippi, about one hundred yards behind the crescent battery on the high road.

This work was executed as a sort of forlorn hope to save New Orleans even for a day. And behind this cut and the ditch the American general, with the most prompt despatch, constructed a barricade of nearly three quarters of a mile in length, extending from the Mississippi on his right to the impassable wood on his left, all across a flat and naked plain, and within a few hundred yards of the British out-guards.

The manner of putting this barricade together was most curious, as in the first instance detached barrels and sugar casks were brought up and left here and there standing isolated, the apertures between them being filled up with mud and all sorts of odds and ends placed along the edge of the ditch so as to form a temporary screen to protect the defenders against musketry; the barricade being hardly breast high, looked like some contemptible expedient, but the ditch ten feet wide and two or three feet deep protected this barricade in front, making a pretty tolerable field position in the first instance.

Four heavy pieces of cannon were now in the crescent battery, which made it somewhat more respectable. The rude barricade as a war stratagem was botched together in a sore straggling way, but was added to and improved in strength from hour to hour, and the interstices betwixt the casks and other crevices of these rough and ready materials were caulked up with mud and other materials first coming to hand. All this labour was executed without any annoyance from the British advanced posts, and actually within one mile and a quarter of their headquarters, by a defeated mass of peasantry, who only stood their ground because no one molested them. And perhaps history affords no example of a similar expedient being executed under such circumstances across a naked plain.

In this state of things, after the landing by the British had been made good for forty-eight hours, Major-General the Hon. Sir Edward Packenham landed, accompanied by Major-General Gibbs, on the 25th, under a fire of balls from the schooner.

Sir Edward taking the supreme command, having been sent from England for that purpose, now examined the plain, which resembled an isthmus or tongue of land, and General Jackson having made a temporary barricade as described from the river to the swampy wood behind the celebrated ditch, now converted the British position into a sort of *cul de sac*.

Sir Edward at once gave vent to his feelings, declaring that troops were never found in so strange a position, the Mississippi from eight hundred to a thousand yards in breadth on their immediate left flank, an impassable wood on the right, within less than three quarters of a mile, the Americans in front, and the fleet only supplying boats to carry off one-third of the force collected on the spot.

Sir Edward augured an ominous result, and every officer and soldier in the bivouac heard these opinions, which were given in no measured terms. The happy moment had passed, but was not irretrievably lost. Notwithstanding these opinions, which had been publicly fulminated throughout the bivouac, and even against this own judgement, Sir Edward declared that as the troops were on the spot he would do his best to get them out of the jeopardy in which he had found them, by persisting in the attack. But strange to relate, Sir Edward failed to make an instantaneous advance, and set himself down to lay siege to the American schooner, the destruction of which, as before stated, had no more to do with the capture of New Orleans than the most foreign thing in nature; besides, a ship with more guns lay higher up the river to dispute the further march on the city by the road, which was no more necessary to take than the sloop in question.

There was no harm in blowing both of them up as soon as possible, but there was no occasion for the whole army to await the event; for while time was lost in disposing of these annoyances, the barricade was rising out of the earth like enchantment as a real stoppage to take the place of an imaginary one.

But putting aside experience in the field, it might have been supposed that not one of these three English generals had ever perused Caesar's *Commentaries*, or had ever contemplated the remains of a Roman camp.

The rapid movements of Napoleon Bonaparte in these modern days were fresh upon the recollection of everyone—did he halt when the enemy were in view, or when winning a victory did he cease to follow it up? But here the rapidity of Bonaparte or the defensive lines of a Caesar were both alike disregarded.

The various houses were not barricaded or loop-holed, nor were trees felled or abattis formed by the British in case of a reverse, for the troops having been brought up as described by driblets in a body, they had no retreat, therefore it behoved the general more particularly to form a stronghold either to give a greater disposable force for attack, to cover any hostile landing that might be made from the right bank of the Mississippi, or in like manner to cover a retreat if necessary.

Here, now, were three British generals, two already having had the supreme command, known for their personal courage in the field, and in the prime of manhood. But all their movements bespoke that their usual energies had succumbed to the trammels of indecision, and to difficulties before them that only existed in their own imaginations.

This square mile was therefore ultimately digged into holes and became the soldiers' burial place without prayers, coffins, or tombstones, and more than five hundred men were put *hors de combat* over and above the original sixteen hundred that landed the first day, and that number alone at first strong enough to have accomplished the conquest in question.

And in the sequel, the deplorable consequences of indecision at this remarkable spot of ground will figure in history and generate the most gloomy sentiments, like those that cross the mind in the sable chamber of death, or while gently drawing aside the velvet pall from the marble-like features of a departed friend, who once smiled in worldly vanity.

It has been proved that General Jackson had not spent his time idly, for in the first instance, having been caught napping, he had shown his profound military and naval skill as a gifted tactician on the night of the 23rd, by counter-manoeuvring and putting the reserve of the British to the very acme of disorder before their front was attacked, a victory which was only lost to the American general owing to the individual bravery of the British veteran troops over his raw levies. General Jackson throughout the operations displayed the art of the engineer, combining at the same time the talent of the wary politician, and the polish of the finished negotiator, and wielding the weapons of war with vigorous decision, and with his pen finally transmogrifying an after defeat to his own advantage.

He had amused the British generals for the space of four days and nights with a blustering fire from the sloop, he had turned every moment to his own account, brought up cannon to the barricades, and caused planking to be laid down for heavy artillery behind the ditch. And although the profile of the crescent battery, and the long line of naked barricade, and its rough exterior face, was not chiselled by the mason, and might have been laughed at by a Vauban, yet the sight of its smoking face caused the British general to halt.

The little British phalanx were again remodelled into two brigades, the one under General Gibbs, consisting of the fourth, twenty-first, and forty-fourth regiments, with the fifth West India black corps. The second, commanded by Major-General Keane, consisted of the eighty-fifth light infantry, the ninety-third Highlanders, the remains of the five companies of the rifle-corps, with the first West India black corps. Colonel Dixon directed the royal artillery, and the squadron of the fourteenth light dragoons not being yet mounted, were employed about the hospitals or other headquarters purposes.

A battery was now scooped out, a quarter of a mile in front of the sugar plantations, for the purpose of heating balls, to relieve the headquarters from the eternal fire of the American schooner. The construction of this battery was judicious, not only for the purposes for which it was intended, but as a check against any more craft from venturing down the river to increase the fire on the bivouac.

But, although the formation of this battery was going on behind the *levée de terre* of the river, still it was no reason why the British force should have been detained from verging along the edge of the forest, to overturn General Jackson's newly raised barricade, or, at least, attempting to do so when in its infancy, in preference to delays, which would only add to its growth, and bring it to strength and maturity.

The 27th, the besieged blew up the American sloop from the battery with hot balls, and her timbers floated down the turbid waters of the Mississippi, but not before her crew had taken to their boats and got safely ashore.

This explosion afforded no small satisfaction to all parties at the sugar plantation, and was hailed by the soldiers as a great relief after a four days irritating and vexatious cannonade, attending them both asleep and awake; the more particularly as the ship took warning at the loss of her consort, and was seen warping higher up the river.

The timbers of the American sloop having well nigh reached the Gulf of Mexico, on the morning of the 28th, at daybreak, General Gibbs, with his brigade, advanced towards the left of the American barricades, and General Keane in like manner along the high road parallel to the river, un-housing an American picket from a building a few hundred yards in front of their crescent battery, which the enemy set on fire to make more smoke.

General Keane's brigade were steadily advancing, the rifle-corps leading, but when within good cannon range, the crescent battery, with full charge of powder and ball, resounded a loud defiance, and some cannon balls, striking the centre of the middle regiment of the British, knocked down the soldiers, and tossed them into the air like old bags. This column, to the utter astonishment of officers and soldiers, was ordered to halt just as their blood was up ready for the usual rush. And the light field-pieces began an interchange with the once insignificant crescent battery.

The American ship of sixteen guns now threw its broadside obliquely in conjunction with the guns of the battery in front, that nearly destroyed all the artillery-men working the two British guns, and soon stopped their remonstrances, which a few sailors finally dragged off the field of contention, the gunners being nearly all killed or wounded. At first, the centre of the column on the high road was thrown into some confusion, but was soon restored to order. The ninety-third Highlanders, from their great steadiness, were the universal talk and admiration, and stood to be fired at as steadily as so many American targets. The brigade were deployed into line, and ordered to lie down, and during the day part of the British troops retired by degrees, both of Gen. Gibbs's and Keane's brigades, leaving the rifles behind to be fired at like so many stumps of trees.

This affair was called, to soften it off, a reconnaissance: these technical phrases are often used in war to cover broader confessions. This reconnaissance, as the phrase went, cost the British well nigh fifty men, principally by grape and cannon shot, without accomplishing any good, and causing a bad morale to creep into the ranks at a time when the superiors were positively forced to promise the soldiers satisfaction, to stop their loud vociferations and complaints at not being allowed to go on. The Americans seeing the backs of the red-coats were elated accordingly, and were almost inclined to make a sortie. Indeed a few shots were fired by the rifles to stop some men in coloured clothes coming out of the barricade, who had advanced beyond the crescent battery.

The headquarters were again established as before, one mile and a half from the enemy's lines. More cannon of heavy calibre were sent for from the fleet, making one hundred and twenty miles going and coming. Admirals Sir Alexander Cochrane, Sir P. Malcolm, and Sir E. Codrington, Captains Sir Thomas Hardy, Sir T. Trowbridge, Sir James Gordon, with others, used the greatest efforts to assist with a ready hand in the superintendence of the bringing up provisions, ammunition, and in conveying to the fleet the maimed and wounded. Most of these officers came up to headquarters, indeed the headquarters of the troops presented a busy scene seldom witnessed in those lonely regions.

The Americans, guessing that they were to be attacked in a formal way, laboured hard at their barricades, and also proved themselves apt scholars after the previous firing of artillery, and so forth; they began to shape their entrenchment into something respectable, but were still obliged to adhere to the direct line of the ditch; but from practice seeing that the face of their barricades should be protected by a cross fire, they established a battery of twelve pieces of cannon on the right or opposite bank of the Mississippi, to enfilade the whole face of their crescent battery, and also across the country, in front of their long line of barricades.

The ship of sixteen guns was warped higher up the river to preclude the possibility of her being fired by hot shot. Large cotton bags were brought in carts from New Orleans of two feet in diameter, and nine in length, to form epaulments, and to flank the embrasures of the American batteries. In fact, no expedient was neglected on the part of General Jackson to profit largely by the long and unexpected truce given him.

A battery having been erected by the British seven hundred yards from the crescent battery of the Americans, on the 1st of January, 1815, His Britannic majesty's troops were again ordered to advance. But a dense white fog for a time obscured all objects, and was one of the luckiest circumstances that could have happened for the advantage of the attacking body. And when it cleared off, the heavy guns of the British opened with such effect, that most of the Americans deserted the crescent battery, and a great deal of confusion happened within their main lines, and this being the first time they had felt the effects of round shot of any magnitude, many of them went off towards New Orleans, and the bravest of them crouching behind their epaulments ready to stand up to repel the expected assault. And for more than ten minutes they did not fire a gun, the British cannoneers having all to themselves. And a whole brigade of infantry close at hand, burned to be ordered on to the assault, and with loud words demanded why they were not led on, when ladders and other materials had been brought up for the passage of that ditch. But to their utter astonishment no such order was given, and there is no doubt that the British troops, rushing on under cover of their guns with a few planks, would have obtained possession of the enemy's works with facility.

The Americans, seeing that no one came to molest them, first opened one gun, then a second, until all their artillery was subsequently manned, when the weak defences of the British mud battery were pierced through and through, some of its guns dismounted, and a fresh batch of artillerymen nearly all killed and wounded; its fire was silenced, and at night the residue of its guns were either dragged away and others buried. The troops were kept again like targets all day, under a galling cross fire from the right bank of the river.

Now what this battery was erected for, unless to cover the assault of the works by the troops, is more than mortal man can explain. For it is well known to infantry that one company would throw up earth enough in a night, squatting down behind which, they would deride all the cannon in Christendom fired by salvos. Thus ended the second siege of the crescent battery.

And would it be believed that night again saw the headquarters of the British at the sugar plantation, a mystery which has never yet been solved?

The American malingerers and the timid, who are always to be found in towns and cities, as well as elsewhere, now crawled up to the barricades, and peeped over the epaulments and the cotton bags thereof, and the very fiddlers and the French horn players from New Orleans struck up their notes within hearing of the British sentinels.

And can it be wondered at that the most extravagant reports flew through the ranks? Amongst others, that the ditch in front of the American lines was a canal, that behind the first line were two others, and the edge of the ditch was proclaimed under the high-sounding title of a *glacis*, and the numbers of the Americans highly exaggerated—nay, that the fortification had existed before the troops had landed at all, and, to crown all, desertion began from the ranks of His Britannic majesty's troops to the enemy.

The British lost in the above useless displays, or whatever they can be called, for I cannot find a name for them, one hundred and forty-two, including officers and men, a greater number, most likely, than would have fallen by sending a storming party of three or four hundred in advance to storm the works at once. Was this not enough to sicken the best troops in the world?

It was now considered by the British general that the American barricade was too strong to attack in front with his present force.

Therefore science was resorted to, and it was proposed to dig a canal of more than a thousand yards in extent, from the head of the bayou or creek, by which the troops had made their landing from Lac Borgne, to communicate with the Mississippi, so that a body of troops should be sent over the river to tread new ground, and to make more demonstrations against New Orleans, although on an opposite side of the river to that on which the city stood.

And this was the state of things fifteen days after the first landing of the British troops; further remarks will be deferred for another place, save that, taking all in all, it did look as though the head, and shoulders, and trunk of the body had emerged from the slough, and that the lower extremities were paralysed and stuck in the mud.

CHAPTER 9

Before New Orleans

After these details the wonder no longer can exist that New Orleans was not a captive city; a sufficient lapse of time had been given the Americans to make their lines impregnable had they deemed fit to do so.

New Orleans was now a military prize of the first class; had it been taken possession of at the onset, the world probably would have only talked or written of it as a dashing marine enterprise, and the British general would have obtained little credit for its capture before its military resources had begun to bud or to expand into notoriety.

General Jackson had shown himself a general of the first class both in attack and defence, since his first surprise. And although so far the Americans possessed the most consummate and able tactician, still the British general commanded the best troops, as they had shown themselves to be on the very ground they now stood upon—and to say that these soldiers were the flower of the British army might invite a controversy; but from discipline and brilliant deeds in the field their conduct could not be surpassed; their ranks were composed of veterans from Great Britain and Ireland, the very elite of His Britannic Majesty's dominions—men who, like the Romans of old, had travailed with pick and spade at batteries and zigzag trenches—men who had fought sanguinary battles in the plain, on the hill, or scaled the mountainside—men who had crowned the deadly breach, or topped the ladder of escalade—men who had forded rivers under hostile balls—men who had fought and starved—men who had starved and fought.

These living targets set up before the elite of the round-hatted Americans, was enough to instil confidence into their breasts, and they had let off cannon and small arms enough to make them ready and willing to do so more effectually from behind their cotton bags, should they be assaulted in right earnest; and those British troops, that had not been in fire before, if they had not been sufficiently baptised at the two whole days' feints in front of the American barricades, must have been endowed with more discipline and patience than fall to the lot of mortality on this terrestrial sphere.

But there was now a further addition of good troops placed on shore who bad not suffered the galling and the unmilitary trials that their fellow-soldiers had been put to, not so much from the losses they had sustained in point of numbers, as being exposed to such slaughter before the enemy, where at each futile attempt the prospect of accomplishing the object in view seemed to diminish, which raised the spirit and the confidence of the defenders on the one hand, while on the other the assailants looked at the difficulties before them as it were through a magnifying glass. For when the doors were left wide open for success, the soldiers were transformed by the wand of authority into automatons, or more properly speaking, into so many statues fresh from the chisel of the sculptor.

The 7th of January, two days after our landing, the first brigade, consisting of the seventh and the forty-third regiments (the two corps mustering under arms upwards of seventeen hundred bayonets) were reviewed in line and within long cannon range, their backs turned towards the enemy's lines.

The music played, the vapour of this swamp had cleared off, the sun shone brilliantly, and the officers and soldiers of these regiments were in the highest spirits at the near probability of their being led on to the attack.

When it was asked why the General-in-Chief, Packenham, did not appear at this review as he was expected, we were told that he was up in a tree in the pine-wood, examining the works of the Americans. Many Peninsular friends of the other regiments were glad to see the seventh and forty-third, and greeted them accordingly; *but what could the Royal Fusiliers and the Monmouthshire Light Infantry do?*

Unquestionably each of these corps carried in their centre the king's standards of crimson, and their regimental colours of blue and white silk, which reminded them of their former renown, and the hard-earned laurels which had been so honourably gained in the Peninsular war; the first corps having served at Martinique, Talavera de la Reyna, Albuera, Badajoz, Salamanca, Vittoria, the Pyrenees, Orthes, and Toulouse, scraps of whose colours, upon its return to England from France, were craved for with outstretched hands, to be honoured with a place in the fair bosoms of the ladies of Devonshire. The second corps were alike recently transported from the fiery ordeal of Vimiera, Corunna, Busaco, Fuentes d'Onoro, Ciudad Rodrigo, Badajoz, Salamanca, Vittoria, Nivelle, Nive, and Toulouse.

The former regiment wore blue facings to their red uniforms, the latter white; one corps used drums, the other bugle-horns; each man carried sixty rounds of ball cartridge in his pouch, and likewise a firelock and bayonet, with extra flints, picker, and brush. The seventh wore a brass plate and white tufts in their caps, and the forty-third

91

wore green tufts and the curved bugle-horn in their's. The former corps carried light blue knapsacks, and the latter black. The officers had swords suspended by their sides, one corps being decorated with gold, and the other with silver ornaments.

But what, I repeat, *could the seventh and the forty-third do without orders,* on the sod of New Orleans? For, after all, they were nothing more or less than machines, *contre eux-mêmes,* or were like a splendid set of chessmen in the hands of those who do not know how to use them, or even prove themselves versed in the common moves of the pawns in default of an adversary making a false move, or when the proper moment arrives to give him check-mate.

In the afternoon of this day the eighty-fifth regiment, which was about three hundred and fifty strong, passed our lines from the front by companies, with intervals between each, as I had seen the light division march in Spain. These companies, though weak, were in excellent order, and proceeded towards the headquarters to be in readiness to embark before daybreak the following morning.

As the eighty-fifth passed along, it struck me that they looked displeased at being removed from the main body, and indeed one or two of the officers so expressed themselves, saying that it would be now our turn to get into New Orleans, as they had done at Washington. This corps had not been fortunate in Spain, and they could not get rid of a mark that had been set upon them, although this regiment had been fresh officered similar to other corps, and remodelled since that time, and when employed had behaved quite as well as other regiments. However, do what they would, "the Peninsular fire-eaters," as they were jocosely called, would give them little or no credit; for, in these days, if a man had not been in half-a-dozen battles, from the effects of which seventy or eighty thousand on either side were swept off, he was designated as "a young hand," and bade to hold his peace, or to be gone with his "subaltern ideas," which naturally suggests the question of how many years the powder-mills are to be kept in requisition, or how many magazines are to be emptied, or where the bowels of the earth are to be ransacked for the supply of iron and lead, and what flints are to be shaped for the trigger before the martial ideas begin to dawn; or whether a pilgrimage to Pompey's pillar is necessary to inspire the warlike writer.

But, after all, the result of a battle seems in the mainspring to be counted more than the quantity of men put *hors de combat,* as the loss of life in the gross is but a sorry recompense without any result, or when both opposing generals writing, or causing to be written, ingenious despatches to their respective governments wherein both claim the victory, and both implore for more ammunition and more "of the golden sinews of war;" the military chest being empty, and not a round left in the soldier's cartridge-boxes, to go at it again with "hammer and tongs."

However, to the point. The eighty-fifth regiment will not be easily obliterated from the archives of America, although certain "Peninsulars" still give them little quarter. When this corps crossed my vista, I must confess that I eyed these soldiers of "Bladensburgh," and of the previous "night combat" already told, with a considerable degree of curiosity.

Some hours after dark so much noise and confusion took place round the headquarters near the canal, that the continued buzz of voices must have been heard in the American lines, added to which several of the huts were in flames. Myself and another officer, being attracted by so unusual a noise, walked to the bank of the river to see whether we could distinguish any lights in the forest on the opposite side of the Mississippi; but everything on the part of the enemy was dark and silent, while on our side confusion, revelry, and mirth prevailed, and we both agreed, on the dyke of the river, that things wore an aspect of an ominous complexion, and, like days mentioned of old, when the rejoicing forestalled the victory.

And we noticed it as a most extraordinary circumstance, that there was no person or sentinel on the bank of the river employed in looking out, and at such remissness we were much astonished. The night was rather dark; and we stood on the *levée de terre* of the river as much alone and undisturbed, although only a short way from the wooden-house, containing the headquarters and the hutted bivouac, as if there had been no troops within an hundred miles of the spot, I may reasonably be asked, how it came to pass that myself and companion were on the look-out more than others.

My friend was a Scotchman, who possessed an amiable disposition, always talking of black grouse, the purple heather of his native Scotch mountains, and was a thorough soldier; and I flattered myself he felt great partiality for my society, as I did for his, and we had often walked together in other warlike scenes and far away from the hum of the bivouac, and in such times might have been mistaken for young antiquaries, as we scrambled up and down the loose stones of the crumbling towers of the mouldering monasteries or the forsaken baronial castles of Europe, or as we looked upwards through the lateral branches of a sheltering tree, with eyes wide open, on many a sleepless night, scanning the twinkling planets, or conjuring up caricature profiles on the half-moon.

My friend did, indeed, love his native hills, and as a proof thereof he carried in his small war-portmanteau a tartan kilt and hose, with red rosette and flaunty garter, and also a handsome dirk, with a broad blade, like those worn by highland chieftains, and withal he could use the Highland claymore, or broad-sword, and would give point most effectively. Here were no toddy arguments or loquacious modern recitals of what the Scotch could do of old; for he would rise from the sod of the bivouac, and stand without flinching upon his guard, and knock aside a sword's cut or thrust with masterly dexterity; and many a day, I, the Englishman, a pupil of a Frenchman, and he, a Scotchman, have, by the hour, stood *vis-à-vis,* the streams of perspiration running down our faces. He loved his country, I say, because he went to live in it as soon as he was released, at the end of a long war, from military duties. And I often used to joke him about the picturesque and tartan highland costume, asking him how it was that the Scotch ever hit upon so splendid a dress?

But to resume. On this eventful night, we both agreed in opinion that there was a looseness and bawling in the sugar-cane bivouac and about the slave huts, which we had never seen or heard before within sight of an enemy and on the eve of an attack; besides these burnings presented a clear sign to the Americans that there was some commotion unusual in our lines, and put them on their guard for a movement of some sort. Further, with a foreboding which proved too ominous in the sequel, we agreed, to use cant phraseology, that there was a screw loose somewhere.

And, moreover, without being accused of speaking of myself imprudently, these, my opinions, may be strengthened by stating that in other countries I had been employed on the look-out post to report the movements of armies larger than the small number of troops occupying the contracted space I now speak of. Therefore, according to such official etiquette, if it goes for anything in America, I may now give my opinion, I trust, without being accused of unpardonable presumption, that, during the whole of the previous day, there had been a downright row in the camp. And it was amusing to see the non-combatants galloping and capering about on short-tailed American hackneys, as though they were bound on some sportive excursion, or collecting names to fill up a handy-cap for some contemplated horse-race; and this gaiety was carried on, and might be observed by the Americans, casting an oblique glance from the tops of the trees just within the left of their lines.

I was always a lover of festive gambols; but the contrast between the past and the coming day was so singularly remarkable, that it calls forth remarks for some of these lotharios, or more properly the leeches of the army, like vultures growing fat upon the carnage of the field of battle, and now prancing about on their American horses, were not to be seen the following day on ground ploughed up, every now and then, by the rusty balls from the American batteries. And there were some strange stories told of certain gentlemen throwing themselves headlong into the boats with the wounded, declaring they were ill, under the care of the doctor, and worn down by dysentery.

Some of the large boats, with carronades in their bows, were lying in the canal, (into which a sufficiency of water had not yet flowed,) which were intended to carry the troops across the river. Standing on its bank, we contemplated the probable result of coming events, and looked with anxiety to descry whether there was any light or fire kindled in the forest on the opposite shore, as the best way of judging whether the Americans were aware of the intended passage of the British troops to that bank of the river, during the night, or as soon as the boats could be got out; but no such indication on the part of the Americans was visible; all in that direction was wrapped in sombre darkness.

My friend and myself having stayed some time at this spot, were of opinion that the Americans were on the opposite bank of the river, or their scouts at the supposed spot of debarkation, but had prudently refrained from kindling any fires, the more effectually to conceal their object.

Whether they were or not, has never transpired to us, as there was no opposition offered near that spot the following morning, upon the landing of the British. But, undoubtedly, the Americans ought to have been there, and might have constructed a battery on that bank of the river, within the distance of little more than one thousand yards of our headquarters, and by a constant fire they would have made the British camp quite untenable, and in this way might have pounded the left of our lines, similar to what was done by the sloop on the first night of landing. And why they did not do so is to this day quite a mystery, unless General Jackson thought that by so doing he should have made the bivouac about the sugar-house so hot by such a shotted annoyance, that the British would have been forced to storm his lines in their own front, choosing that attempt as the least of two evils, and in preference to a perpetual cannonade; for if they retired, they only got into a swamp, and if they advanced they were within range of the American lines.

I had scarcely reached the bivouac from the bank of the river, and was about to lie down to take some repose, when I was ordered to join two hundred soldiers of my own corps at eleven o'clock at night, for the purpose of marching to the front to mend and guard a battery, within seven hundred yards of the right of the American lines—in fact to the very spot close to the high road leading to New Orleans, where the British had hesitated and twice recoiled from the effects of the American artillery.

As soon as we had reached this dilapidated mud redoubt,

within point-blank range of the American crescent battery, both in front as well as from the batteries on the right bank of the river, spades were put into the hands of the soldiers (while others kept guard) to endeavour to make it tenable before daylight, but as the water sprang up at the depth of a foot or nine inches below the surface of the soft ground, the men were obliged to pare the surface for a great extent round, and to bring the shovels and spades dropping with mud to plaster on the queerest entrenchment I ever saw. In this fashion we laboured the latter portion of the night. And some pieces of cannon were dragged with exceeding toil, by the soldiers and sailors, to place in battery. But the time would not permit all the platforms to be laid down. And, indeed, its epaulements were not cannon-shot proof. The want of materials and the short time allowed, made it impossible to make them so. Here I first met Lieutenant (afterwards Captain) West, of the Royal Engineers, a most accomplished, zealous, and intelligent officer.

Some time before daybreak I noticed the forms of men silently gliding past the right of the temporary battery, and on approaching I found them to consist of some of the rifle-corps who were going to the front to take up their ground, to watch the American lines, to form a chain of posts, and to be in readiness to open their fire *à la point de jour*. These riflemen were gliding along with the same silent footsteps as they were wont to do, on the eve of so many memorable occasions where their services had been required.

Probably no troops that ever stood under arms could boast of having taken up so many dangerous and venturous posts, and of having been so often in close contact with an enemy without being detected, or without making any un-necessary noise in their ranks, or causing a lonely shot to be discharged at them, owing to an enemy having been pre-maturely alarmed. The out-posts, during the silent hour of night, give rise to a variety of solitary thoughts. How often have we seen the day close, and kept watch together during the hours of the tempest, on the snow-covered ground, as well as on those brilliant nights in Spain, when the broad shadows of the morn lighted up the soft and tranquil scenery, to lull the imagination with the most alluring thoughts and associations of the "past, the present, and the future."

When people talk of the field of battle, and the heat of the fight, how little do they know how many tedious hours the troops of outpost duties have to undergo, waiting for the whispers or the tread of an armed foe, or in momentary expectation of a flash of fire, or a discharge of bullets, and how often these troops are exposed to straggling and single combats for whole days. This was the case with the rifles, for they had always been in front, and always called for, and before New Orleans were much cut up.

These troops took up their ground according to orders, and were ready to attack as soon as the signal was given, but were extended in a useless way, and ranged along a front to be exposed singly to an overpowering are, instead of leading the front of the small column destined to attack the detached half-moon battery on the right of the enemy's lines or barricades.

I do not remember ever looking for the first signs of daybreak with more intense anxiety than on this eventful morning; every now and then I thought I heard the distant hum of voices; then again something like the doleful rustling of the wind before the coming storm, amongst the leaves of the foliage. But no, it was only the effect of the momentary buzzing in my ears; all was silent—the dew lay on the damp sod, and the soldiers were carefully putting aside their entrenching tools, and laying hold of their arms to be up and ready to answer the first war call at a moment's warning.

How can I convey a thought of the intense anxiety of the mind, when a solemn and sombre silence is broken in upon by the intonation of cannon, and when the work of death begins. Now the veil of night was less obscured, and its murky mantle dissolved on all sides, and the mist was sweeping off the face of the earth; yet it was not day, and no object was very visible beyond the extent of a few yards. The morn was chilly—I augured not of victory, an evil foreboding crossed my mind, and I meditated in solitary reflection. All was tranquil as the grave, and no camp-fires glimmered from either friends or foes.

Soon after this the two light companies of the seventh and ninety-third regiments came up without knapsacks, the Highlanders with their blankets rolled and slung across their backs, and merely wearing the shell of their bonnets, the sable plumes of real ostrich feathers brought by them from the Cape of Good Hope, having been left in England. One company of the forty-third light infantry also followed, marching up rapidly. These three companies formed a compact little column of two hundred and forty soldiers, near the battery on the high road to New Orleans.

They were to attack the crescent battery near the river, and if possible to silence its fire under the muzzles of twenty pieces of cannon; at a point, too, where the bulk of the British force had hesitated when first they landed, and had recoiled from its fire on the 28th of the last December, and on the 1st of January. I asked Lieutenant Duncan Campbell where they were going, when he replied, "I be hanged if I know."

Then said I, "you have got into what I call a good thing; the far-famed American battery is in front at a short range, and on the left this spot is flanked at eight hundred yards by their batteries on the opposite bank of the river." At this piece of information he laughed heartily, and I told him to take off his blue *pelisse* coat to be like the rest of the men.

"No," he said gaily, "I will never peel for any American—come, Jack, embrace me."

He was a fine grown young officer of twenty years of age, and had fought in many bloody encounters in Spain and France, but this was to be his last, as well as that of many more brave men.

The mist was slowly clearing off, and objects could only be discerned at two or three hundred yards distance, as the morning was rather hazy; we had only quitted the battery two minutes, when a Congreve rocket was thrown up, but whether from the enemy or not we could not tell; for some seconds it whizzed backwards and forwards in such a zigzag way, that we all looked up to see whether it was coming down upon our heads. The troops simultaneously halted, but all smiled at some sailors dragging a two-wheeled car a hundred yards to our left, which had brought up ammunition to the battery who, by common consent as it were, let go the shaft, and left it the instant the rocket was let off. This rocket, although we did not know it, proved to be the signal to begin the attack. All eyes were cast upwards, like those of so many philosophers, to descry, if possible, what would be the upshot of this noisy harbinger, breaking in upon the solemn silence that reigned around. During all my military services I never remember seeing a small body of troops thrown at once into such a strange configuration, having formed themselves into a circle, and having halted, both officers and men, without any previous word of command, each man looking earnestly as if by the instinct of his own imagination to see in what particular quarter the anticipated firing would begin, canopied over as these soldiers were with a concave mist beyond the distance of two hundred yards, was impossible to solve.

The Mississippi was not visible, its waters likewise being covered over with the fog; nor was there a single soldier, save our own little phalanx, to be seen, or the tramp of a horse or a single footstep to be heard by way of announcing that the battle scene was about to begin, before the vapoury curtain was lifted or cleared away for the opposing forces to get a glimpse one of the other. So that we were completely lost, not knowing which way to bend our footsteps, and the only words which now escaped the officers were "steady, men; steady, men," these precautionary warnings being quite unnecessary, as every soldier was, as it were, transfixed like fox-hunters, waiting with breathless expectation and casting significant looks one at the other before Reynard breaks cover.

All eyes seemed anxious to dive through the mist, and all ears were attentive to the coming moment; as it was impossible to tell whether the blazing would begin from the troops who were supposed to have already crossed the river, or from the great battery of the Americans on the right bank of the Mississippi, or from their main lines. From all these points we were equidistant, and within point blank-range; and were left, besides, totally without orders and without knowing how to act or where exactly to find our own corps, just as if we had not formed part and parcel of the army.

The rocket had fallen probably into the Mississippi; all was silent, nor did a single officer or soldier attempt to shift his foothold, so anxiously was the mind taken up for the first intonation of the cannon to guide our footsteps, or as it were to pronounce with loud peals where was the point of our destination, well knowing that to go further to the rear was not the point to find our regiment.

This silence and suspense had not lasted more than two minutes, when the most vehement firing from the British artillery began opposite the left of the American lines, and before they could even see what objects they were firing at, or before the intended attacking column of the British were properly formed to go on to the assault.

The American artillery soon responded with their cannon, and thus it was that the gunners of the English and the Americans were firing through the mist at random, or in the supposed direction whence came their respective balls through the fog. And the first objects we saw, enclosed as we were in this little world of mist, were the cannon balls tearing up the ground and crossing one another, and bounding along like so many cricket balls through the air, coming on our left flank from the American batteries on the right bank of the river, and also from their lines in our front.

At this momentous crisis a droll occurrence took place, a company of blacks emerged out of the mist, carrying ladders, which were intended for the three light companies of the left attack, but these Ethiopians were so confounded at the multiplicity of noises, that without further to do they dropped the ladders and fell flat on their faces, and without doubt, had their claws been of sufficient length, they would have scratched holes and buried themselves from such an unpleasant admixture of sounds and concatenation of iron projectiles, which seemed at war one with the other, coining from two opposite directions at one and the same time.

To see the ladders put on the shoulders of these poor creatures, who were nipped by the cold, excited our greatest astonishment, knowing that it requires the very elite of an army for such an undertaking; for soldiers that will place ladders under a heavy fire are capable of anything, as it requires the most desperate efforts to lug them along over broken ground, ditches, and other obstacles, the men all the while falling from the effects of the enemy's balls; sometimes one end of the ladder comes to the ground without supporters, and then the other. For if the difficult operation takes place in the daytime, the enemy point all their engines of destruction at those carrying the ladders; the troops are excited; those that are left rush forward to grapple with difficulties not to be surmounted without assistance, at a time when the supporters of the ladders have let them drop, irritated and suffering from the pain of their wounds, others having fallen to rise no more. And probably out of ten or twenty ladders only two or three out of the whole can be raised against the enemy's parapets.

On the other hand, if such an operation takes place at night, the least obstacle stops the progress of those carrying them, the soldiers fall, the ladders lay upon the ground, and are lost during the dreadful confusion. These evils in war are out of the pale of all theory. The operation must be seen to be well understood; and I know of no rule except by selecting men of the most tried courage, and gifted with the most persevering and undaunted resolution, and if they fall, the operation must be left to the energy of the storming party. But taken as a whole, it is one of the most difficult of all enterprises, and of this the practical engineer officer is aware as well as myself, having seen in Spain and elsewhere the difficulty of raising ladders against walls, when well opposed, and also the great numbers dropped and left lying about even by the most veteran troops.

If these blacks were only intended to carry the ladders to the three light companies on the left, they were too late. The great bulk of them were cut to pieces before the ladders were within reach of them; even if the best troops in the world had been carrying them, they would not have been up in time. This was very odd, and more than odd; it looked as if folly stalked abroad in the English camp. One or two officers went to the front in search of some responsible person to obtain orders *ad interim;* finding myself the senior officer, I at once, making a double as it were, or as Napoleon recommended, marched to the spot where the heaviest firing was going on; at a run we neared the American lines. The mist was now rapidly clearing away, but, owing to the dense smoke, we could not at first well distinguish the attacking column of the British troops to our right.

We now also caught a view of the seventh and the forty-third regiments in echelon on our right, near the wood, the Royal Fusiliers being within about three hundred yards of the enemy's lines, and the forty-third deploying into line two hundred yards in echelon behind the fusiliers. These two regiments were every now and then almost enveloped by the clouds of smoke that hung over their heads and floated on their flanks, for the echo from the cannonade and musketry was so tremendous in the forests, that the vibration seemed as if the earth was cracking and tumbling to pieces, or as if the heavens were rent asunder by the most terrific peals of thunder that ever rumbled; it was the most awful and the grandest mixture of sounds to be conceived; the woods seemed to crack to an interminable distance, each cannon report was answered one hundred fold, and produced an intermingled roar surpassing strange. And this phenomenon can neither be fancied nor described, save by those who can bear evidence of the fact. And the flashes of fire looked as if coming out of the bowels of the earth, so little above its surface were the batteries of the Americans.

We had run the gauntlet, from the left to the centre in front of the American lines, under a crossfire, in hopes of joining in the assault, and had a fine view of the sparkling of the musketry, and the liquid flashes from the cannon. And melancholy to relate, all at once many soldiers were met wildly rushing out of the dense clouds of smoke lighted up by a sparkling sheet of fire, which hovered, over the ensanguined field. Regiments were shattered, broke, and dispersed—all order was at an end. And the dismal spectacle was seen of the dark shadows of men, like skirmishers, breaking out of the clouds of smoke, which slowly and majestically rolled along the even surface of the field. And so astonished was I at such a panic, that I said to a retiring soldier, "have we or the Americans attacked?" for I had never seen troops in such a hurry without being followed.

"No," replied the man, with the countenance of despair and out of breath, as he ran along, "we attacked, Sir."

Still the reverberation was so intense towards the great wood, that anyone would have thought the great fighting was going on there instead of immediately in front.

Lieutenant Duncan Campbell, of our regiment, was seen to our left running about in circles, first staggering one way, then another, and at length fell on the sod helplessly upon his face, and in this state several times recovered his legs, and again tumbled, and when he was picked up he was found to be blind from the effects of a grape-shot that had torn open his forehead, given him a slight wound in the leg, and had also ripped the scabbard from his side, and knocked the cap from his head. While being borne insensible to the rear, he still clenched the hilt of his sword with a convulsive grasp, the blade thereof being broken off close at the hilt with grape-shot, and in a state of delirium and suffering he lived for a few days.

The first officer we met was Lieutenant-Colonel Stovin, of the staff, who was unhorsed, without his hat, and bleeding down the left side of his face. He at first thought that the two hundred men were the whole regiment, and he said "forty-third, for God's sake save the day!"

Lieutenant-Colonel Smith, of the rifles and one of Packenham's staff, then rode up at full gallop from the right, (he had a few months before brought to England the despatches of the capture of Washington,) and said to me, "did you ever see such a scene? There is nothing left but the seventh and forty-third! Just draw up here for a few minutes to show front that the repulsed troops may re-form." For the chances now were, as the greater portion of the actually attacking corps were stricken down, and the remainder dispersed, that the Americans would become the assailants. The ill-fated rocket was discharged before the British troops moved on; the consequence was, that every American gun was warned by such a silly signal to be laid on the parapets ready to be discharged with the fullest effects.

The misty field of battle was now inundated with wounded officers and soldiers who were going to the rear from the right, left, and centre; in fact, little more than one thousand soldiers were left unscathed out of the three thousand that attacked the American lines, and they fell like the very blades of grass beneath the scythe of the mower. Pakenham was killed, Gibbs was mortally wounded, and his brigade dispersed like the dust before the whirlwind, and Keane was wounded. The command of His Majesty's forces at this critical juncture now fell to Major-General Lambert, the only general left, and who was in reserve with his fine brigade.

With the exception of the two hundred soldiers under my orders, in the centre there was hardly a man formed all the way to the bank of the Mississippi, or any reserve ready to resist, for nearly the space of half a mile of ground which was immediately in front of the whole of the right and the centre of the American barricade, or to hinder them from dashing up the high road to the canal and the place where Colonel Thornton had embarked with his force, for the passage of the river.

Had the Americans only advanced, the probability would have been by this movement that they would have got one mile behind the seventh and the forty-third regiments, and the fugitives that had retired into the swampy wood; and had they succeeded in beating back the soldiers under my orders, and some sixty or seventy soldiers under the orders of Lieutenant Hutchinson of the Royal Fusiliers, who clung round the left battery, after retreating from the crescent battery, when he found nearly all his men killed or wounded, and that the principal attack had utterly failed, and himself left without any support.

The rifle-corps individually took post to resist any forward movement of the enemy, but the ground already named being under a crossfire of at least twenty pieces of artillery, the advantage was all on the side of the Americans, who in a crowd might have completely run down a few scattered troops exposed to such an overpowering force of artillery.

The black troops behaved in the most shameful manner to a man, and, although hardly exposed to fire, were in utter and abominable consternation, and lying down in all directions, and amongst them the white feather nodded triumphant. One broad beaver with the ample folds of the coarse blanket thrown across the shoulders of the American was as terrible in their eyes as a panther might be whilst springing amongst a timid multitude. These black corps, it was said, had behaved well at some West India islands, where the thermometer was more congenial to their feelings.

Lieutenant Hill said, in his shrewd manner, "Look at the seventh and the forty-third, like two seventy-fours becalmed!"

As soon as the action was over, and some troops were formed in our rear, we then, under a smart fire of grape and round shot, moved to the right, and joined our own corps, who had been ordered to lie down at the edge of a ditch; and some of the old soldiers, with rage depicted on their countenances, were demanding why they were not led on to the assault.

The fire of the Americans from behind their barricade had been indeed most murderous, and had caused so sudden a repulse that it was difficult to persuade ourselves that such an event had happened—the whole affair being more like a dream, or some scene of enchantment, than reality.

And thus it was: on the left bank of the river, three generals, seven colonels, seventy-five officers, making a total of seventeen hundred and eighty-one officers and soldiers, had fallen in a few minutes.

The Royal Fusiliers and the Monmouthshire Light Infantry, from the beginning to the end of the battle, were astounded at the ill success of the combat, and while formed within grape-range were lost in amazement at not being led on to the attack, being kept as quiet spectators of the onslaught.

Lieutenant Augustus D'Este, of the Royal Fusiliers, and aid-de-camp to General Lambert, rode up to our regiment, his countenance full of animation, declaring that he had never enjoyed himself more, and protesting that he would rather hear the balls whistle through the air than the finest band of music. These expressions were so un-Orleans like, that I fail not to note them down.

About an hour and a half after the principal attack had failed, we heard a rapid discharge of firearms and a few hurried rounds of cannon on the right bank of the river, when all was again silent, until three distinct rounds of British cheers gladdened our ears from that direction, although at least one mile and a quarter from where we were stationed. They were Colonel Thornton's gallant troops, who were successful in the assault on the American works in that quarter, the details of which, for a brief space, I must postpone.

For *five* hours the enemy plied us with grape and round shot; some of the wounded lying in the mud or on the wet grass, managed to crawl away; but every now and then some unfortunate man was lifted off the ground by round shot, and lay killed or mangled. During the tedious hours we remained in front, it was necessary to lie on the ground, to cover ourselves from the projectiles. An officer of our regiment was in a reclining posture, when grape-shot passed through both his knees; at first he sank back faintly, but at length opening his eyes and looking at his wounds, he said, "Carry me away, I am *chilled to death;*" and as he was hoisted on the men's shoulders, more round and grape-shot passed his head; taking off his cap, he waved it; and after many narrow escapes got out of range, suffered amputation of both legs, but died of his wounds on board ship, after enduring all the pain of the surgical operation, and passing down the lake in an open boat.

A wounded soldier, who was lying amongst the slain two hundred yards behind us, continued without any cessation, for two hours, to raise his arm up and down with a convulsive motion, which excited the most painful sensations amongst us; and as the enemy's balls every now and then killed or maimed some soldiers, we could not help casting our eyes towards the moving arm, which really was a *dreadful magnet* of attraction: it even caught the attention of the enemy, who, without seeing the body, fired several round shot at it. A black soldier lay near us, who had received a blow from a cannon-ball, which had obliterated all his features; and although blind, and suffering the most terrible anguish, he was employing himself in scratching a hole to put his money into.

A tree, about two feet in diameter and fifteen in height, with a few scattered branches at the top, was the only object to break the monotonous scene. This tree was near the right of our regiment: the Americans, seeing some persons clustering around it, fired a thirty-two pound shot, which struck the tree exactly in the centre, and buried itself in the trunk with a loud concussion. Curiosity prompted some of us to take a hasty inspection of it, and I could clearly see the rusty ball within the tree. I thrust my arm in a little above the elbow-joint, and laid hold of it; it was truly amusing between the intervals of firing the cannon, to witness the risks continually run by the officers to take a peep at this good shot. Owing to this circumstance, the vicinity of the tree became rather a hot berth; but the American gunners failed to hit it a second time, although some balls passed very near on each side, and for about an hour it was a source of excessive jocularity to us.

In the middle of the day a flag of truce was sent by General Lambert to General Jackson, to be allowed to bury the dead, which was acceded to by the latter on certain conditions.

And now having given all that came under my observation in the centre of this curious fight, probably it will not be amiss, during the flag of truce, to offer some general details of much more consequence than what was seen by myself; and in the whole some repetition may appear on the face of my pages, yet I know not how. To break in upon the scene of fire and smoke, and all the lofty associations of the battle-field with the cold details of plans which were laid down by the British general, which in no one instance were acted upon.

CHAPTER **10**

Disaster

The eighty-fifth light-infantry regiment, with armed sailors and marines, and the first West-India corps of blacks, in all twelve hundred men, were making the greatest exertions, during the night, to get the boats out of the canal, to cross to the right bank of the Mississippi river before break of day, and endeavour to seize sixteen pieces of cannon, most of which pointed across the Mississippi, and by their fire raked all along the front of the American lines about to be attacked by the main body of the British. But, owing to the canal not being cut sufficiently deep, or the river falling lower than was expected, many of the ships, barges and pinnaces were aground, and only a number sufficient to convey across the river seven hundred men, could be got out just before daybreak; and thus consigned to the Mississippi, with muffled oars, these soldiers vanished from the anxious glances of the British general.

Upon the success of these troops hinged the main attack on the American lines; and if Colonel Thornton succeeded in mastering these batteries, he was to turn the cannon upon the Americans, when the British main body was to move on to the assault on the left bank of the river.

But owing to the boats being aground in the canal, daylight broke before this force could land on the opposite side of the river, which totally altered all the plans laid down: it behoved Sir Edward Packenham to wait patiently until the success of those crossing the river was known. The silence which reigned around was a happy harbinger that all went on well, as the great probability was that the British troops might have been fired on from the right bank of the river, before or while getting out Of the boats.

Although day had broke, still a sort of fog hung upon the surface of the earth, and the British, general might have withdrawn his front columns, which were formed within seven hundred yards of the American lines, with the utmost ease and facility, and then have quietly waited to see the upshot of those sent across the river.

The forty-fourth regiment, four hundred strong, were broken up, one hundred to form a covering party, with three companies of the rifle-corps, and the remainder to be employed in carrying fascines and ladders for the purpose of facilitating the passage of the remainder of the troops across the wet ditch; and so flat was the country in its front, that it was difficult to see this breast-work a short way off.

The attack upon the Americans was to be made as soon as break of day or twilight made objects at all visible, and those of the New World could be distinguished, as, owing to their speaking English, much confusion had taken place at the night attack on the previous 23rd of December; and it was thought better to fight them in broad daylight, when their want of discipline would not be shielded under the cover of darkness.

The forty-fourth regiment and the twenty-first Royal North British Fusiliers were to lead the attack in columns, to be supported by the fourth or King's Own. This column was composed of two thousand men.

The ninety-third regiment of Highlanders were to be a

moveable column to threaten the centre of the American lines, or to act as circumstances might require, and the surplus of the five companies of the ninety-fifth or rifle-corps were to be extended along the front of the left and left centre. Some light troops were to endeavour to turn the extreme left of the American long line of entrenchments. In this wood the tribe of savages ensconced themselves.

The light companies from the seventh Royal Fusiliers, the ninety-third Highlanders, and one company from the forty-third light infantry regiment, were to attack the often-mentioned crescent battery, without any support, under the mouths of twenty pieces of cannon; and singular to recount in the annals of the military world, at the precise spot at which the main body of the British had hesitated *twice before* when in an *unfinished* state; but which entrenchment had now grown into and was the very iron horns of the American position. This little column consisted of two hundred and forty British.

The seventh Royal Fusiliers and the forty-third light infantry regiments were to compose the reserve, and to support, if necessary, the principal column of attack. The third West-India regiment of blacks were also in reserve.

The American position, as before stated, was now formidable, and the only chance of taking it was, by getting as near as possible under cover of darkness, and then by a bold rush gain the edge of the ditch before the Americans could begin a heavy firing.

The canal had been cut a thousand yards in length, broad and deep, from the head of the creek, and making an acute angle three hundred yards from the river, ran direct into it. This work was worthy of a Roman general, and the indefatigable labour of his cohorts; and had there been a breastwork thrown up behind, it would have constituted a position of ten times the strength of the lines of the Americans.

Under the mask of this canal the British general, if necessary, might have continued on the defensive against the world in arms, while, feeding and succouring, from time to time, those that had already crossed the river, and within one mile and a half of the American lines, he could have debouched to attack at midday, should the result across the river prove fortunate. There was no time to be lost, as the Americans, like the ancients, entrenched, barricaded, and re-entrenched, according to passing exigences.

With such a position, then, the British general could have no fear of evil results, while making a wide movement to the left by water. This is even supposing his columns of attack were ready to assail the American lines in front, which they were not; his orders had been disobeyed, the few troops intended for the attack were not ready to go on either on the right or the left; for neither party had been supplied with proper necessaries for crossing the ditch.

By some mistake the officer commanding the forty-fourth regiment had passed the redoubt during darkness, where the ladders and fascines were scattered about for his use, and indeed had halted alongside of it for ten minutes without an engineer officer coming forth, or even sending a message after the regiment when it had gone on. But the question is, was any engineer officer present at this time to do so? It always is customary, on such occasions, for the engineer not only to point out these things in person, but to see that his directions are implicitly obeyed; and a commanding officer even of a regiment is only a secondary person when the engineer department comes into requisition on such occasions.

In all the sieges at which I have been present, the very conspicuous part taken by the engineers generally was so remarkable and indefatigable, that there cannot be a second opinion on the subject. Nay, what is more remarkable, a sergeant of the Royal Artillery even stepped out of this redoubt, and acted as a guide during the darkness to the forty-fourth regiment, to the advanced battery, within seven hundred yards of the American lines; and this mistake might easily have been made by the officer commanding the forty-fourth, as *redoubt* and *battery* are synonymous.

How was it that this mistake was not rectified, with staff-officers enough for ten times the number of troops present?—that no one found out this fatal error until too late to rectify it? It would be conjectured that the troops having been twice baulked at this very spot, those whose duty it was to superintend ought to have been on the *qui vive.* And, indeed, the troops could hardly know whether they were going on in earnest or not; and this was shown beyond all dispute when the attack did begin. And it is no less strange than true, that the two hundred and forty soldiers in front of the crescent battery were precisely in the same predicament; not a fascine or a ladder for their use was brought up when they rushed on to the attack. Moreover, two hundred soldiers of the forty-third regiment, who had been working at a battery all night within close range of the crescent battery, as already stated were at daybreak without orders, and when dismissed by the engineer, knew not which way to bend their footsteps for the purpose of joining their regiment.

The forty-fourth regiment was ordered back *(nearly three hours after they had taken up their ground)* more than a quarter of a mile for ladders and fascines at daybreak, having lost their breath with running and hurrying. Half these soldiers had not gained their proper position in front of the column of attack; hence they were hurried into action, and opened out, struggling as they were to place fascines and ladders across a ditch in face of some of the best marksmen in the world, and at broad daylight.

Sir E. Packenham was now on the bank of the Mississippi, listening and waiting the result of the passage of the boats about one mile and a quarter from his front columns of attack; in fact, in a central position, to order the main attack on his own side of the river to go on or to be checked. But he was now no longer his own master, as he could not see the troops under his own command; and it behoved him to wait, to give his own plans time to develop themselves. A thick mist hung on the ground and over the river, which was most fortunate for the plans of the general, as the Americans could not see the boats passing across the river, nor the columns of attack, within so short a distance of their main lines.

Here was *la fortune de la guerre* fully exemplified; for, owing to the delay of the boats, daylight had already appeared, and two hundred yards every way could be clearly seen; and had it not been for the mist, as a matter of course the Americans would have opened fire, both on the boats as well as the columns formed for the intended main attack. The mist proved the most lucky screen possible, and really made amends for the want of water in the canal, which prevented the boats getting out earlier.

Now it must be clearly understood, that part of the troops, with Herculean labour, toiling knee-deep, like navigators, and covered with mud for a week, while cutting the canal, were the soldiers who twice before, from superior orders, had retired from the *exact spot* at a time they all thought they were going on, and who were led to believe, while excavating the canal so long as eight days before, that the American works had become too strong to attack in front, and that they were making this passage by way of turning these works. Fifty armed boats were brought up from the fleet. In short, everyone was on the tip-toe of expectation; every eye was turned towards the right bank of the river; and all was quiet.

It was impossible to know what obstacles the troops might not meet with while landing, what abbatis might be thrown across the forest ways, and what creeks or inlets might not stay their march, even had they made good a landing. But the silence which existed was a good omen: not a cannon, not a single musket had been discharged from either side of the river: therefore there was nothing to bewilder or throw the British general off his guard in the excitement of the moment; when, wonderful to recount, and lamentable to detail, Sir E. Packenham declared that he *"would wait his own plans no longer"* and commanded that the fatal, *the ever-fatal rocket* should be discharged as a signal for the forty-fourth, twenty-first, and fourth regiment to begin the assault on the left of the American lines; thus, at one fell swoop, all chances of success were thrown, as it were, to the bottom of the river.

The mist was slowly clearing away; and, to add to other misfortunes and other injudicious arrangements, three hundred men of the forty-fourth, who were to lead the attack, were only clearing a redoubt five hundred yards behind the head of the column, at whose head they ought to have been, with shouldered ladders and fascines, when this rocket was let off.

The consequence was, that everything was disorganized before a shot was fired; the British artillery began to fire, and were soon answered by those of the Americans. The column was impelled onwards, the twenty-first leading, followed by the fourth regiment, and the soldiers of the forty-fourth carrying fascines and heavy ladders, all round the column, while puffing and blowing from their previous running back to the redoubt for the ladders.

As this column neared the American lines, the musketry opened on them while crossing the drains which here and there intersected these flats; and as there was not the least cover, the troops began to suffer much, and then hesitated within a hundred yards of the lines, and opened a heavy fire of musketry, which positively obliged the rifles which led to cling to the earth.

And now the baneful effects of past occurrences burst forth in the most glaring colours. A cry sprang up from the rear of the column, "Retire! Retreat! There is an order to retreat!" At this critical moment Sir E. Packenham rode up from the banks of the Mississippi; and Major-General Gibbs, in despair, declared that the troops would not follow him. The musketry of the enemy increased.

General Gibbs was mortally wounded, and, with imprecations on his lips, was carried off the field. Sir E. Packenham, now taking off his hat, rode to the head of the column, and valiantly cheered on the soldiers, who were falling and staggering like drunken men from the effects of the fire, some going back and others going on. Here Sir E. Packenham was wounded in the knee, and had his horse slain under him; and while mounting a second charger, the brave general received his mortal wound, and fell dead into the arms of the aid-de-camp.

The confused column soon gave way on all sides. Major-General Keane was also wounded; and a few brave officers and soldiers were prowling about at the edge of the ditch, in vain waiting for only a few planks and some support to enable them to enter the American works; lieutenant Lavack and some straggling soldiers of the twenty-first did actually get in, but were obliged to surrender themselves prisoners.

The remains of the column now took shelter at the edge of the swampy wood, or behind the redoubt, totally disorganized. By some strange error, which still remains a mystery, and perhaps ever will, the ninety-third Highlanders being isolated, were marched up within good musketry range of the American lines, instead of supporting the three victorious companies on the high road, and being then ordered to deploy into line, stood like statues, until they had lost in killed and wounded, including those that fell of their light company, five hundred and forty-four soldiers; and the residue of the regiment, of about three hundred, were obliged to vacate the field.

The two light companies of the seventh Royal Fusiliers, the ninety-third Highlanders, and the one of the forty-third light infantry, soon after the firing of the British artillery had begun, rushed forward under a murderous fire of cannon, rifles, and other small arms; and although the crescent battery was defended bravely, muzzle to muzzle, by some of the American regulars of the seventh regiment, the New Orleans rifle company, and also by some Kentucky riflemen, and notwithstanding the obstinate defence, the British soldiers, with fixed bayonets, forced themselves into the battery by one of the embrasures, the very moment after a cannon defending it had been fired.

The Americans that were driven out of this battery were seen to run across a single plank close by the river to get into the extreme right of their main line of entrenchments, which were only a short way behind the battery. The defenders stood to their guns to the very last moment; and Lieutenant-Colonel Renny, of the twenty-first Fusiliers, who was placed in the command of these three companies, was shot by a merchant of New Orleans, while hanging over the entrenchment of the battery.

At the moment of reaching this battery the ranks of these soldiers were well nigh crushed and annihilated; for eight officers and one hundred and eighty men out of the previous two hundred and forty were extended killed and wounded; and when the remainder took the battery, the Americans only gave ground because the attackers were seized with a frenzy.

This handful of soldiers tenaciously clung to the battery, and the four pieces of cannon were taken, by ensconcing themselves in its exterior ditch, (as the interior of the redoubt was open and exposed to the fire from the main lines of the Americans,) in hopes of some further succour coming to them; and it was only when the grand attack had failed that they thought of retreating, which was effected by some of the soldiers raising their caps on the points of their bayonets, and making a shout, which induced the enemy to fire a volley, and before the smoke had cleared away these intrepid soldiers at full speed were almost out of musketry range. It has been erroneously asserted that some of these troops even reached the main line of the enemy's entrenchments, but this was not the case.

The only three officers that escaped unwounded were Lieutenant Hutchinson, of the seventh Fusiliers, who had three shot-holes through the right side of his cap, or more properly speaking six, counting the egress made by the balls behind his cap; Lieutenant Lorentz, of the same regiment, had the back of his white shoulder-belt almost cut in twain with a musket-shot; and Lieutenant Steele, of the forty-third, was the only officer who had escaped without a score or a mark of any sort.

Thus it was that the moment of victory eluded our grasp, owing to the loss of General Sir E. Packenham, who undoubtedly would have pushed forward the reserve, and decided the fate of the day. The seventh Fusiliers and forty-third regiment were formed in echelon within less than *six hundred yards* of the enemy, filled with enthusiasm, and waiting impatiently in vain for an order to force a passage; but there they stood, idle spectators of the direful defeat, after having been brought *so many thousand miles* to join in the combat. Had they been moved forward, the fortune of the day would have been effectually restored and the victory clenched.

Captain Wilkinson, acting brigade-major to General Gibbs, had his horse shot under him, but with an eagle eye he saw the Americans slackening fire, and rushed forward on foot; a ball pierced his body, and he fell into the shallow ditch, mortally wounded, and while gasping for breath, said to the only officer who had accompanied him, "*now*, why do not the troops come on? *The day is our own.*"

Lieutenant Lavack, of the twenty-first Fusiliers, then scrambled up the earth entrenchment, and seeing the enemy flying in a disorderly mob, demanded the swords of two American officers, who at the first impulse were surrendering themselves prisoners; but, on recovering their self-possession, and finding the gallant English officer unsupported, they replied, "Oh, no; you are alone, therefore ought to consider yourself our prisoner:" and on looking over the parapet, Lieutenant Lavack found to his unutterable astonishment that the British troops had receded, and in a manner declined taking advantage of the proffered boon.

Lieutenant Lavack, two months afterwards, when released at the conclusion of the war, (with two shot-holes through the plate of his cap,) declared before seven of us, that the whole of the Americans on the left of their lines had run away, with the exception of the two beforementioned officers. During the ardour of the battle this gallant officer sprang over the mud-works; and while describing the whole proceedings to us, said, "Now, conceive my indignation, on looking round, to find that the two *leading regiments* had vanished, *as if the earth had opened and swallowed them up.*" These were the exact expressions used by him.

As soon as the smoke had cleared away, the transatlantic citizens that had got into a melee of confusion, finding that the left of their lines was not taken possession of, recovered their self-confidence, and re-trod their footsteps to re-man the lines. At the commencement of the fusillade the Americans made great havoc in the ranks of the British, owing to the precision of their fire.

During the heat and the smoke of the firing, the Americans got entangled one with the other, and were in the most extraordinary confusion, while crowding their parapets eight or ten deep; and as the front men let off their pieces, and fell back to reload, to make place for other aspirants "to take a shoot" as they called it, those that had fallen back were afraid to return to the parapet; and it is a singular fact, that during the *mêlée*, both hostile bodies were flying one from the other at the same time, but under very different circumstances; the British having well nigh lost two thousand men, whilst their opponents, ensconced up to their chins, had only sustained a loss of some fourteen persons killed and wounded—a circumstance unparalleled in modem history.

Although the loss had been so great on the part of the British, and a decided repulse had been given to their columns, still the reserve were anxiously looking for the result of the attack of Colonel Thornton on the other side of the river; thinking that, if he was successful, the reserve, backed up by the troops already repulsed, would make some further attempt.

More than an hour had elapsed since the attack had first begun; and the cannonade was pretty brisk, both from the front and on one flank from the batteries on the right bank of the Mississippi, which did little injury, as the cannoneers could not see us, owing to the dead level. All at once we heard, on the other side of the river, *pop, pop, pop,* followed by a volley of musketry, interspersed with a few hasty rounds of artillery, which ceased as suddenly as it had begun, and every one spontaneously said "Bravo! The batteries are taken, and the Americans are done for."

The troops in the boats had been carried a little down the stream of the river, owing to the great force of the current, and under cover of the fog had landed unopposed a short way farther down than was intended. However, as soon as they had formed their ranks, and heard the great convulsion of sounds going on at the principal, attack, they hurried on to a temporary bridge across an inlet, drove the American picket before them, and coming in front of an unfinished entrenchment, were received by a very heavy volley. The sailors and marines for a moment were taken aback, but Colonel Thornton, taking off his hat at the critical moment, with his regiment not four hundred strong (backed by the marines and sailors), by a sort of charge of skirmishers at the point of the bayonet, took all the American works, their batteries, with sixteen pieces of cannon and one stand of colours of the New Orleans militia, with the small loss of seventy-eight men; the eighty-fifth losing forty-three, the marines sixteen, and the armed sailors nineteen.

Twelve hundred Kentucky, Tennessee, and other Americans, under General Morgan, flew from the field without looking behind them, and without sustaining hardly any loss. So swiftly did they vacate their entrenchments, covered by their own smoke, that they hardly gave the victors time to climb the bank, to get a shot at their retreating footsteps.

This panic is easily accounted for; the British attacked, as they were wont to do, by rushing into the enemy's smoke, which, clearing away, only showed the red coat and yellow facings triumphant, and the eighty-fifth light infantry again ran away with the American laurels, which they so well deserved, in the same manner as they had done at Bladensburgh. And although they were well supported by the sailors and marines, yet all the credit was due to the eighty-fifth leading the van, and answering the spontaneous call of Colonel Thornton, who was wounded. And singular enough, these victorious troops thought that the grand attack had succeeded, although only half a mile from the extreme right of the American entrenchments.

We waited and waited, still exposed to a cannonade from the front, and in our turn expected to hear all the captured guns open fire and enfilade the American entrenchments from right to left, exactly in the same way that the American sloop had raked the English bivouac on the first night of landing; but no such agreeable sounds greeted our ears, the Americans having spiked their guns on the right bank of the river before they were taken possession of.

But still Colonel Thornton had accomplished everything that was desirable, or that the most sanguine expectations could have contemplated. And although Sir Edward Packenham was no more, his ultimate plans had been realized by the able conduct of Colonel Thornton, who had seized the happy instant of making his successful charge.

Had all the generals brought their troops into action like Colonel Thornton and Lieutenant-Colonel Renny, a most brilliant conquest would have crowned the enterprise, would have added new lustre to the British arms, and closed this bloody war by a glorious achievement, as worthy of record as it is now unworthy.

Ten armed boats, with carronades in their bows, floated on the waters of the Mississippi, and forty more boats were ready to follow them, if necessary, and batter the right flank of the Americans to the very portals of New Orleans, who did not possess a flotilla to engage them.

The British troops now swept the right bank of the Mississippi, and were ready to move on within eight hundred yards of New Orleans, and might on that side have built another city of the same name, had they been so inclined. General Jackson had lost more than half his artillery, and his troops were in the utmost dismay and confusion within their lines, and there was nothing left to save them, except by making a bold rush to try to seize the boats still aground in the canal, cut by the British, which they did not attempt to do. The repulse they had met with in the night of the previous 23rd of December, by the troops that first landed, had produced such an effect on their minds of the impracticability of an open warfare, that they made no attempt to sortie beyond the crescent battery and line of entrenchments.

General Lambert's reserve were as cool as cucumbers, and joking one with the other; the repulse in front, in the eyes of these old soldiers, was not considered decisive. The British general possessed two batteries within seven hundred yards, opposing the right and left of the American entrenchments. Besides which, in case of being overpowered by numbers, he had the canal at his back, which nothing could cross, and he had the long wished-for command of the mighty waters of the Mississippi, and all the assistance that a powerful fleet could give, and still within five miles of New Orleans, and seventeen hundred troops not yet engaged, burning for the onslaught, and wishing by fresh efforts to wipe off the stain cast upon His Majesty's uniforms.

Here was a glorious position! Here was another opening to the streets of New Orleans, and dame Fortune soared aloft in favour of the English general.

Chapter 11

Truce

In this position, wonderful to recapitulate, a flag of truce was sent to General Jackson by the British general, at the very time such a proposition might have been expected from the opposite quarter, to ask the American general leave to bury the dead who were now lying under his lines; which truce General Jackson gladly acceded to, and embraced with the utmost eagerness, provided the British general would consent not to send any reinforcements across the river: nay, he even consented to refrain from doing so himself, so glad and rejoiced was he of any hopes of gaining time to extract by some great effort such a thorn stuck into his side. And, moreover, so intent was General Jackson to gain time during such an unlooked-for respite, that, as a lure, he permitted the British fatigue parties to approach nearer to his lines than he had ever done before, without throwing a curtain of smoke from his artillery to hide their weak parts from scrutiny.

At midday, a line being drawn at a few hundred yards from the lines, the Americans handed over from different points the dead bodies of about three hundred British soldiers, many of them naked, having been stripped of their uniforms, to be hawked about the streets of New Orleans in triumph, or the caps placed on the heads of Americans, and the tufts and feathers of officers and soldiers stuck into their round hats as trophies of this day. And while the British soldiers were digging holes to bury their dead, the Americans picked up one thousand stand of small arms, left by the killed or dropped by the wounded men, of the King's Own, the Royal Fusiliers, the North British Fusiliers, the forty-fourth, the forty-third Light Infantry Regiment, the ninety-third Highlanders, and the ninety-fifth or rifle corps.

About three hundred of the wounded soldiers of the above corps were also carried into the American lines as prisoners; and these prisoners were looking for momentary, relief from captivity, owing to the success on the right bank of the river; but they were not rescued, but abandoned, to bite their nails with deep chagrin at the broad jokes of the Americans, who recovered their self-possession as soon as it was known that the British troops had of their own accord given up their great victory on the right bank of the river.

While the interment of the slain was taking place, the Americans in front, when they found out by this flag of truce the great extent of our loss, which they did not know before, were so elated, that some of them indulged in many jests and jibes; but to their credit let it be admitted that the wounded, when once within their lines, were treated with the greatest humanity, put into good houses, and their wants supplied with unsparing hand.

During the rest of this gloomy, raw, and cloudy day, we maintained our position without budging an inch to the rear; and at seven o'clock in the evening saw a great conflagration on the other side of the river, on the extreme right of the American lines. We retired two hours after dark to the original ground the troops had marched from in the morning; and when we found that Colonel Thornton's troops had been withdrawn from the opposite side of the river, and re-landed, and that the boats were again got into the canal, then, and not till then, all further hopes of victory were blasted.

At such a piece of information it is impossible to convey an adequate idea of our astonishment at such an advantage being given up. But this was only the finale of the many fantasies played off on the banks of the Mississippi to confound the "god of war," and to bring the many inexplicable contrarieties since the first landing to the climax. Never before this had I felt that inferior officers and soldiers were nought but machines, when this last piece of well-earned good fortune was flung away for the feast of carrion birds of prey: and His Majesty's uniforms held up or cuffed about in derision; and every button, and every breastplate, and every thread eyed with the scrutiny of American curiosity.

Was this not enough, I say, to make His Majesty's officers hold hard the breath of suppressed indignation at being reined in when so much blood had been spilled, and when the words of their dying comrades still called on them to advance? And to quote General Jackson's own brief expressions will throw additional light on this most extraordinary of all hesitations: for when an opposing general makes such a candid and honest confession as is here made, and that too the very day after the affair, what can be more conclusive?

General Jackson having, in a dispatch to the Hon. James Munroe, secretary-at-war, dated January 9, 1815, four miles below New Orleans, briefly detailed the repulse of His Britannic Majesty's troops, and having taken five hundred prisoners, and stated the small loss sustained by the Americans, goes on to say:

> The entire destruction of the enemy's army was now inevitable, had it not been for the unfortunate occurrence which took place on the other side of the river.

Simultaneously with his advance on my lines, he had thrown over, in his boats, a considerable force to the other side of the river. These having landed were hardy enough to advance against the works of General Morgan; and what is strange, and difficult to account for, at the very moment when their entire discomfiture was looked for with a confidence approaching to certainty, the Kentucky reinforcements, on which so much reliance had been placed, ingloriously fled, drawing after them, by their example, the remainder of the forces, and thus yielding to the enemy that most fortunate position. The batteries which had rendered me for many days the most important service, though bravely defended, were of course now abandoned; not, however, until the guns had been spiked.

This unfortunate route had totally changed the aspect of affairs. The enemy now occupied a position from which he might annoy us without hazard; and by means of which he might have been enabled to defeat, in a great measure, the effect of our success on this side the river. It became, therefore, an object of the first consequence to dislodge him as soon as possible. For this object all the means in my power, which I could with safety use, were immediately put in preparation.

Perhaps it was somewhat owing to another cause that I succeeded beyond my expectation. In negotiating the terms of a temporary suspension of hostilities to enable the enemy to bury their dead and provide for the wounded, I had required certain propositions to be acceded to as a basis; among which this was one—that, although hostilities should cease on this side of the river until twelve o'clock of this day, yet it was not to be understood that they should cease on the other side, but that no reinforcements should be sent across by either army until the expiration of this day.

His Excellency Major-General Lambert begged time to consider of these propositions until ten o'clock of today, and in the meantime re-crossed his troops. I need not tell you with how much eagerness I immediately regained possession of the position he had thus hastily quitted.

The enemy having concentrated his forces, may again attempt to drive me from my position by storm. Whenever he does, I have no doubt my men will act with their usual firmness, and sustain a character now become dear to them.

Chapter 12

Retreat

January 9th, the army had taken up its original position, but still maintained its outposts within musketry range of the American lines, who amused themselves by throwing shot and shell generally at midday and also at midnight. Although the distance was one mile and a quarter, still they contrived to elevate their cannon, so that the balls sometimes flew over us or lobbed into our frail huts, and the heavy shells from a large mortar dropped amongst us in a similar manner, but the ground was so soft, being composed of alluvial soil, that whenever the shells reached it without exploding, they seldom did any injury, merely making large holes of five or six feet deep, then bursting with a dead sound and scattering the loose mould.

At this spot the water did not spring up so near the surface as in the vicinity of the American lines, which could not be approached by zigzags as at ordinary sieges, owing to the water springing up at the depth of a foot. From the time we landed, I did not see a stone or pebble of any sort, and as if the birds were aware of this, they would hop within a few yards of us without taking flight. These flocks consisted of birds very like robins, their breasts being of a reddish tint, but they were much larger than a blackbird. The Americans, hearing our martial music, seemed resolved to give a response, and every morning before daylight played several tunes with a band of music that was stationed about the centre of their lines, and one particular waltz was seldom omitted.

Three days after the attack, a grave was dug for Lieutenant Duncan Campbell of our regiment, who expired in great agony from the wound in the head, and being sewed up in a blanket he was consigned to a clayey resting place. An officer stood at the head of the wet grave reading the funeral service, with a prayer-book in his hand; the rest of the officers were standing round the grave with caps off, when a shell from the enemy came whistling through the air, and was descending apparently upon our heads, but fortunately it exploded one hundred yards in the air with a dreadful crash, showering down a thousand iron fragments, which we heard dropping in every direction, without injuring one of us. The noise having subsided, the prayer was then concluded, the grave covered over, and we retired from the solitary ceremony.

The night after this burial a shell exploded over a hut in which two officers of our regiment were sleeping, which cut off both the feet of Lieutenant D'Arcy—the one just below the knee, and the other at the ankle-joint, and he crawled out of the hut in this horrible situation. One of his feet was driven so far into the soft mould that it was obliged to be dug out the following day.

A round shot knocked the cooking kettle off a fire, which was encircled by officers' servants, without doing further damage than spilling the soup, which in these hard times was a very serious inconvenience; for owing to adverse winds and the necessity of carrying the wounded down to the shipping by Lake Borgne, a distance of sixty miles, and bringing up in return provisions, the sailors were quite exhausted. They had been exposed for more than a month in the depths of winter to all kinds of weather, sweating on the oars by day, or perishing with cold in the open boats by night. The consequence was, that the consumption was beyond the produce; on some days we did not taste food, and when we did, it was served out in such small quantities as only to tantalize our voracious appetites, so that between short commons and a perpetual cannonade, we passed ten days after the repulse in as uncomfortable a manner as could fall to the lot of most *militaires* to endure.

One morning before daylight we were disturbed (having been kept awake half the night by the usual salutations of shot and shell) by the water pouring into our huts, and as soon as objects could be discerned, what a dreary prospect presented itself to view! The Mississippi had over-flowed its banks, and nothing but a sheet of water was to be seen, except a few straggling huts and one house, the lines of the Americans, and the forest trees. It was nearly dark before the waters subsided. The whole day the troops were enveloped in muddy blankets, shivering with cold, as hungry as hunters, and looked like polar bears standing on their hind legs. The enemy, who were as badly off as ourselves, ceased firing, being, as we afterwards understood, up to their knees in mire.

One day being in advance on picket in a fort constructed by the parings of the black-loam for some twenty or thirty yards around, and within a few hundred yards of the enemy, I distinctly saw with my telescope a motley group of Americans traversing and elevating a gun, for the purpose of throwing lob-shot over our heads into the principal bivouac. One of these civil artillery-men was capped with a red woollen cap, a second wore the hat of a miller, and so on. The epaulements of the embrasures, which I could clearly distinguish, were supported by round packs of cotton, eight or nine feet long and two in diameter.

A grove of the loftiest orange-trees I ever saw grew near

the scattered houses, and were covered with oranges nearly ripe; this may appear surprising at this season of the year, but such was the case; and in lack of other food we cast them into iron pots half filled with sugar, mixed with a little water, by which process we converted them into candied orange-peel, which in some degree satisfied the cravings of hunger, but brought on complaints, added to the cold and wet, which sent many officers sick on board ship. The sugar in the hogsheads was crystallized with the alternate rains, frost, and the occasional gleams of sunshine, and ate very like candied sugar.

A day or two before the brigade of field artillery were put on board the boats (which took place during the night), some straw was loosely strewed over the guns that their departure might not be noticed by any of the negroes wandering about the houses, and to prevent them giving any information to the enemy that we were about to de-camp. The old ship-guns were abandoned, and left in the advanced batteries as trophies to the Americans.

On the 18th it was intimated that we were to retire dur-ing the night. At eight o'clock in the evening another offic-er and myself were hanging over the dying embers of our fire on the extreme left of the lines, in readiness for the or-der, to move off. All fires were extinguished, when the flash of a cannon disturbed our meditations by sending a whiz-zing round shot from the opposite bank of the Mississippi into our bivouac; a second and third salutation plunged so near that we raked out the small fire to throw the enemy off the range, and the soldiers were so irritated that they fell in simultaneously, and demanded to be marched to the front or to the rear. I never saw the troops more indignant; they vociferated in loud sneers at the whole process of the operations, and it was truly amusing to hear the quaint re-marks of some of these hardy veterans.

At nine o'clock we silently filed off to enter a marsh which had never before been traversed by human footsteps, except those of the engineer officers, who had been superintending the cutting down of reeds and placing boughs of trees at the most boggy places, to endeavour to make something like a road for the infantry to pass, there not being a sufficiency of boats to carry off the troops in a body. Fortunately the weather held up; otherwise, had a heavy fall of rain happened during the march, we must all have perished in the slough.

As a matter of course the few horses and other materials appertaining to the army had been previously conveyed on board ship. For a short way we proceeded on the hard road, following the preceding column, and then entered the swamp, and the first step sank up to the knees in mud, and we continued to drag one leg after the other, sometimes falling on our faces, and at others sinking in up to the hips, and anyone unluckily stepping off this road was almost certain of going over head and ears. At one spot the men came to a dead stop; an officer, more valiant than wise, pushed everyone aside and boldly stepped forward to lead the way; but courage availed him little, for in an instant he was up to his neck, and had it not been for the timely exertion of those present, in two seconds he would have disappeared.

The soldiers were obliged to carry their firelocks in both hands horizontally, so that when they lost their footing, they might hang to their arms until assisted by their comrades. During the whole of the night we scrambled and tumbled about in this bog, and when morning broke, a scene presented itself which beggars all description. The straggling files of the soldiery extended along the quagmire for miles, enclosed by high reeds; every countenance was plastered with mire; in fact, the whole army were covered with a cake of mud from the top of the head to the sole of the foot, and to increase the agreeables of this most extraordinary of all marches, the air was darkened by flights of wild ducks, and a dead alligator nine feet in length lay across the way. The monster had been despatched by the thrust of a bayonet in the belly, and one of its forelegs was broken by a Herculean blow; each leg was nearly twice as thick as a man's arm. The back and tail of these amphibious animals are covered with a dark shell like a coat of mail, which is musket-ball proof.

At ten o'clock the following morning we reached a place of rest called the Fishermen's Huts, which stand on an artificial ground, but surrounded by a swamp or spongy morass, rising four or five inches above the surface of the creek, and therefore subject to frequent inundations. Here we passed some wretched days upon half allowance, without any fuel, save the reeds, to kindle fires which flared up with a puff, and went out in an instant, without conveying any warmth to our shivering bodies. Here an officer of the rifle-corps shot a wild duck with a single ball, and this duck without sauce was so much talked of, that I really believe half the troops dreamed of this *bon morceau.*

Two launches, armed with carronades in their bows, were pushed up the creek, to prevent any of the enemy's boats from coming down suddenly upon us; otherwise our position was impervious, as there was no possibility of reaching us, it not being very likely that the Americans would voluntarily enter the swamp by which we had marched from necessity. A night or two before we quitted this place, the enemy landed near these boats to make a reconnaissance, but two rounds of grape-shot and some musketry from a picket of our regiment, under Lieutenant Hill, obliged them to decamp,

I passed a night near this post—and such a night as I shall not easily forget; a hut composed of propped reeds stood close to the creek, and just before dark I saw an alligator emerge from the water, and penetrate the wilderness of reeds which encircled us on this muddy quagmire as far as the eye could reach. The very idea of the *monster* prowling about in the stagnant swamp took possession of my mind in a most forcible manner—to look out for the enemy was a secondary consideration. The word was, look out for *alligators!* Nearly the whole night I stood a few paces from the entrance of the hut, not daring to enter, under the apprehension that an alligator might push a broad snout through the reeds and gobble me up. The soldiers slept in a lump. At length, being quite worn out from want of sleep, I summoned up courage to enter the hut, but often started wildly out of my feverish slumbers, involuntarily laying hold of my naked sword and conjuring up every rustling noise amongst the reeds to be one of these disgusting brutes, with a mouth large enough to swallow an elephant's leg.

Captain Sir James Gordon, of the Royal Navy, who commanded the *Seahorse* frigate, took up his station at the Fishermen's Huts, to superintend the embarkation of the troops by detachments. This spot was the grand gossiping rendezvous. Lieutenant Steele, of our corps, inclined to the amphibious, was always joking with him of the *Seahorse;* and, being vastly fond of everything appertaining to shipping, took up a paddle which belonged to a canoe, and quietly walked off with it into the bog, and then waited, that Sir James might see him, who instantly called out, "Halloo, you sir, you have got one of my paddles!"

"Well, I know that," was the reply: "I have no firewood, therefore I am going to cook my dinner with it."

Captain Gordon jumped up, but having a wooden leg, the stump stuck in the mud, and an armistice was entered into between this true cut of a sailor and the soldier, amid roars of laughter. Lieutenant Steele was to help Sir James out of the mud, and to surrender the paddle on the condition that Sir James would supply him with a dinner. The two days we remained here the weather was pretty fine. Some black slaves had preceded us to these huts, with the hope of escaping from their masters, and were assembled to dance for our amusement, accompanied by a sort of rude pipe and tabor. The negroes went through violent contortions of countenance, by grinning, and throwing the head first on one side, then on the other, raising their knees in unison, kicking out their legs with the utmost elasticity, and throwing out their arms and snapping their fingers; but the style of the negresses was the most singular; they only shuffled with their heels, without shifting their ground, in a manner hardly perceptible without the most exact scrutiny, and always fronting the negroes; but, instead of using the feet, as in other countries, they moved and beat time to the music with the muscles of their posteriors in the most exact manner—a practice, no doubt, taught from their infancy, as no other part of the frame moves except that *projecting part*.

On the morning of the 25th of January we quitted the morass. The ship's barge I was in conveyed nearly fifty men, and was rowed by twelve men-of-war men; and, had I not been present, I never could have believed that sailors, with ponderous oars, could have continued such exertions for so many successive hours; now and then the naval officer called out, when they appeared to *"Flag, hurra! Hurra! Give way!"* which seemed to cheer their drooping spirits and renovate their declining strength. Thus, after twenty days' bivouacking, and with rotten shoes, we were put on board the *Bucephalus* frigate, anchored off Cat Island.

The day had been very fine, and while in conversation with a full-grown midshipman on the extraordinary manner a boat's crew of Americans had contrived to kidnap and make prisoners three officers and fifty privates of the fourteenth Light Dragoons while they were comfortably snoozing and covered with a tarpaulin, as they were passing down the lake one night, for the purpose of going on board the shipping—amongst other things I asked the midshipman what sort of a captain he was under, when he answered, "Sir, are you not aware that a captain of a man-of-war is a king?—Well, then, my captain is king of kings."

CHAPTER 13

L'Isle Dauphin

In a few days the fleet weighed anchor, and steered its course, with gentle breezes, towards Mobile Bay, and in twenty-four hours dropped anchor opposite L'Isle Dauphin, where the troops disembarked early in February, and were put under tents.

The soldiers no sooner landed than they dispersed themselves amid the thickets of pine and cedar trees, and began a hot fusillade at the few cattle and hogs appertaining to a Mr. Cooney, of Irish extraction, who had been banished to that island for some misdemeanour committed in the American navy, in which he informed us he held the rank of midshipman. Himself and wife were its only inhabitants, although it was some miles in length, and from one to three in breadth. Before any order was issued, the soldiers, who had been for months on salt provisions, had destroyed every four-footed animal they could get a shot at; the consequence was, when all the mischief was committed, an order was promulgated that no more were to be destroyed. This meat was so rank, and tasted to such a degree of rushes, which the cattle fed on, that it was impossible to stomach the flesh until well salted down, and even this process would not effectually take away the unpleasant flavour of the rushes. The Americans occupied a small fort, on a sandy promontory, at the mouth of Mobile Bay, but after two or three days' cannonade it capitulated, with its small garrison of four hundred men.

The side of the, island on which we were stationed was three hundred yards from the shore, of a dry sandy soil, but as it abounded with alligators and numerous other reptiles, great care was taken to clear the ground of the underwood, and ditches were dug round our tents to prevent the nocturnal visits of the *alligators,* which lay dormant at this time of the year, although a stray one would sometimes protrude its enormous head and fore-legs out of a stagnant pool, to bask in the rays of the sun, or would creep, with a rustling noise, through the underwood; and at a short distance they resembled a piece of burnt timber.

In a few days almost the whole of the tents were hidden from view, and the labyrinths of the camp presented a most picturesque appearance, as every tent was enclosed by a wickerwork fence, interwoven with quantities of the richest evergreens, representing all the intricacies of a handsome plantation.

In this island of natural productions there are birds of the most beautiful plumage, such as humming-birds, parrokeets, eagles, pelicans, and various other species which fluttered in the trees, forming a perfect aviary. The shores abounded with delicious fish and extensive oyster-beds; the marshes produced wild fowl and large snipe, and its sands generated snakes, scorpions, and other reptiles; and, although it was considered by us a pleasant situation, Mr. Cooney informed us that during the warm weather a European would be nearly devoured alive, of the authenticity of which I had certain proof before we left it.

Here we found a spot encircled with pine trees, round which seven of us formed a wickerwork fence of great solidity, and also dug a ditch of considerable width, which measured ninety-five yards in circumference; in the interior huts were constructed of the cedar-tree and other odoriferous shrubs. It was named Fort Anselmo, and *au centre* blazed an enormous fire; around its bright blaze we happily caroused.

Amongst other inconveniences attendant on long voyages, provisions at this period began to fail the fleet, and for many days scarcely any biscuit was served out; our breakfast consisted of chocolate without sugar, fat pork, cut into rations and burnt over the embers of the fire, to serve as bread to the oysters.

One night, while seated round the crackling wood fire, a negro slave, who had escaped from his master or driver, and accompanied us from before New Orleans, said, "Massa, I see little cow!" a piece of intelligence which made us prick up our ears, and each seizing a musket, we sallied forth, and, when close to General Keane's oblong wickerwork hut, (—he had nearly recovered the effects of his wound,—) the black pointed out a calf; a volley was discharged; it fell; but, to our consternation, it was found to be tied to a stake by the leg, clearly indicating it to, be private property. To be detected would never do: our cook therefore sprang forward, threw the animal on his back, and hid it in our fortification of wickerwork.

The whole camp was in alarm at the report of the firearms; the guards were flying in all directions; many of the soldiers turned out and stood to their arms, under the supposition that the enemy had made a descent; and, to add to the joke, the general, a day or two after, invited one of our mess to breakfast with him, who broke four eggs, out of six, into a tumbler, with pepper and salt, and swallowed them. "Well," said the General, "if that is not the most light-infantry way of eating eggs I ever saw: now really I should not wonder if some of you young gentlemen have not purloined my calf;" which, by-the-bye, was now cut into chunks and crammed into pork-casks, and this pickled veal was subsequently distributed to our particular friends as a rarity. But this was not all, as one depredation begets another.

An officer came back from a tedious day's sport; being without small shot, he could not bag any game, and seeing a cow grazing near the shore, he shot her through the head with a bullet, and covered the carcase over with evergreens, and had scarcely reached home before a great outcry arose amongst the sailors in search of the Admiral's milch cow, which, in due time, was brought in, salted down, and presented to some of the fusiliers as rations.

An enormous pine-tree, stripped of its bark and lower branches, to the height of at least sixty yards, stood a mile from our camp, towering and completely overtopping all the other trees of the forest. On the top of this, the most stately tree that I ever beheld, and amidst the branches, which only tufted round its highest altitude, a silver eagle had built its nest,, which we were determined to possess ourselves of; and as there were no means of getting at it without felling the huge tree, with a numerous party, we repaired to the spot and set to work, and, after much toil and most exceeding labour, when it was sufficiently cut with the axe and numerous bill-hooks, ropes were affixed round the trunk, and, after tottering, it came down with a tremendous crash, so much so, that although I was stationed a distance of an hundred yards from its base, firing ever and anon at the eagle, which hovered in the air at least a quarter of a mile over the nest that contained her young—yet, when the prodigious tree fell towards me, I involuntarily shrunk and tottered backwards, and at the same time coming in contact with the root of a shrub, I lost my equilibrium, and measured my full length at the same moment with the tree, still frightened, and keeping my eye fixed on the falling mass, whose broken branches flew about in every direction with the concussion.

One of the young eaglets had its neck broken, but the other was uninjured. They were just fledged, and were about the size of a half-grown goose; the nest was very large, about the bulk of a common clothes' basket, and was composed of branches of trees, most of which were the circumference of a person's finger, and the whole of them were very dry and brittle.

The same day an officer shot an alligator in the top of the head with a musket-ball while the monster was basking in the sunbeams with its head just above the surface of the water, in a stagnant pond within the limits of our camp ground. It was some hours before the vital spark was entirely extinct. Two young alligators, each measuring more than a foot in length, were kept in a tub of water, and whenever put close together with a stick, no matter how often during the day, they would fight in the most vicious manner.

One night a soldier's wife was nursing her child in a hut by the light of a taper, when a huge alligator crawled in, looked about, and then slowly backed its horrible shelled carcase out again, the poor woman all the time clasping her infant in her arms and transfixed with horror and consternation, in momentary expectation that the amphibious monster would devour herself and child.

As a sort of explanation of a sham partisan warfare that took place in Dauphin Island, I must state that while in Spain a troop was formed bearing the title of "Britannia's Hope," or the "Defenders of Innocence;" and each knight armed with a lance assumed a name such as Florian of the Desert, Palmarin of England, Sebastian of Spain, Amadis de Gaul, and so on. I also took the title of Don Anselmo, and probably a more ludicrous scene than that which occurred on the day of its formation could not have taken place. The spot selected for the ceremony was a small amphitheatre enclosed with trees in full blossom. Each cavalier having decorated himself and horse with branches of blossom, dismounted to have his colour presented to him from my hands, consisting of an old bandana handkerchief which was tied to a pole, the whole of the knights joining in chorus "God save the King." We then mounted our horses and went our way in search of adventures, myself being dubbed with the honorary appellation of captain of the troop. But to revert to our sham warfare in America, where the greater portion of the officers of six regiments with might and main were eagerly engaged, and also the officers of the dismounted squadron of the fourteenth Light Dragoons, with as much zeal and anxiety as if the fate of a capital city was to be decided on the eventful day of a pitched battle, when two armies were about to begin the work of death face to face. Orders for this petty war were issued in writing, despatches were sent backwards and forwards by night and day: some of the autograph copies I still hold as specimens sent to me as the honorary Commander-in-Chief of one of the two rival and partisan camps.

To the best of my belief this very amusing and interesting little guerrilla warfare in truth originated about the egress to and fro to a broad path or opening which was overshadowed by trees on each side, and situated behind the lines of the eighty-fifth Light Infantry, where peradventure a pair of bright eyes and a feminine costume, which had been recently imported from England, were to be seen. This broad walk was known to a few as a "by-word" of Pall Mall, in allusion to the great lounging street of that name in England's overgrown metropolis.

On the ground and under the pine trees was strewed a very great abundance of cones or pine-tops of considerable size, many of them being seven or eight inches in length and as many in circumference, and when soaked through by the rain or immersed in water they were of goodly weight, and when thrown with force and exactitude, gave and left marks on the physiognomy of an ugly character. Of the effects of these cones I can speak feelingly, having received four black eyes at different times during the various onsets and skirmishes which happened in the course of the two months that we were in the labyrinth of trees and the wickerwork encampment, where from the height of enclosures and fences the red spiral tops of the white canvas tents were hardly visible in some places above them.

There was a long open space of three hundred yards in breadth, (which was called the plain,) separating the two woods, in one of which the seventh Fusiliers and the forty-third were under canvass or hutted. On the other side of the open space were the eighty-fifth, ninety-fifth (rifles), the ninety-third Highlanders, and also the fortieth regiment, which had recently arrived in this island. The already described Pall Mall was nearly in rear of these last named regiments, who soon declared themselves as our opponents, from a reconnaissance made by some of our light troops for the ostensible purpose of negotiating an amicable treaty to admit of a free ingress and egress to their promenade of Pall Mall.

On one side of the broad path which led from an encampment, the eighty-fifth had a sort of advanced wickerwork enclosure, which in a manner flanked the direct way (called the high road) to Pall Mall, The consequence was, that after some recon-noitering and parleying, the van-guards of the eighty-fifth and the forty-third, the latter being on their way to Pall Mall, began a rapid encounter with pine-cones, and seeing from some sand-hills that my van-guard, although victorious in the plain, were unable to penetrate into their labyrinths of wickerwork and strong-holds, I marched with a chosen body to their succour, and without a halt stormed the above fort by a small breach which was now the bone of contention, took it, and therein hoisted our colours as soon as it had surrendered at discretion. Amadis de Gaul, my second in command, and who had been hotly engaged from the beginning of the onset, and while the fort was in his charge, sent me the following despatch, and although not emanating from official organs, still this despatch describing the sham fight is penned so like many real despatches, of course of much greater moment and importance, that I cannot resist the temptation of inserting it as a relic the most *recherche* of our younger frolics. It will be detected by the nature of the despatch that brevet ranks were bestowed with unsparing hand, and that a staff was formed as it were by sleight of hand, rough and ready, and were as expert at the pen, plucked from the pinions of the eagle or the vulture, as though they had been old stagers and grown grey in the service. This precious *morceau* runs verbatim as follows:

Isle Dauphin
March 3, 1815
Sir,—I beg leave to report to your Excellency the particulars of the action with the enemy this morning before your arrival. Having formed my division, I received orders from your Excellency to advance and reconnoitre the enemy's out-post. I did so, and found them totally unprepared for the attack. I advanced with caution some distance into their lines, but the alarm being given by a few skirmishers of the enemy, they soon collected a force of more than double ours, which obliged me to fall back and take up a position within musket-shot of their advanced fort. The enemy, having from his magazines plenti-

fully supplied himself with ammunition, advanced to attack us. We allowed them to come close to us before we opened our fire, which did great execution in the enemy's ranks. Colonel Carroll, at the head of his brigade, made a most gallant charge on a very superior body; but owing to the great superiority of the enemy, Colonel Carroll's brigade were obliged to retire. Seeing this, I ordered the brigade of M'Lean's to charge, and led them myself. While going on I was several times wounded, as were several of the brave brigade at whose head I was, but the impetuosity of our charge was not to be withstood, and the enemy gave way in every direction, leaving two prisoners and Colonel Carroll, whom they had taken from us. They then threw a brigade into the fort, while with the remainder of their army they defended their right flank. I made several attempts to take the fort with my division, but owing to the great superiority of the enemy, could not succeed until your Excellency's arrival with a reinforcement, when our brave army carried everything before them.

I feel particularly indebted to Colonels Carroll and M'Lean for their assistance, and the very excellent dispositions they made with the brigades they commanded. I also beg leave to mention my aid-de-camp Captain Hill. In fact no encomiums of mine can do justice to the bravery of the officers and soldiers under my command. I beg leave to enclose a return of wounded. I have the honour to be
Your Excellency's most obedient servant,
Amadis de Gaul
General of division
To Don Anselmo, Commander-in-Chief, Fort Anselmo

The captured fort was of no use to us, being at too great a distance from our encampment to garrison it; however it was thought best to retain it for twenty-four hours as a trophy of our prowess. A treaty was drawn up between myself and Captain Travers of the rifle-corps, who commanded the army of our opponents, as follows:

Sunday

The fort to be made in the same state as it was prior to our being attacked, subject to the inspection of both parties. Thus it will remain in the possession of the forty-third forces.

The forty-third and seventh who were inside the fort today, when we retired, to remain there until twelve o'clock on Monday. An exchange of prisoners as formerly.

(Signed) *Travers*

Field Marshal

Commander-in-Chief of the allied army

Camp Fort Impracticable

(Granted) *Anselmo*

Commander of Forces, Fort Anselmo

After this, various encounters and combats took place, and both parties set to work to strengthen their works and entrenchments; but the two formidable citadels opposed to one another were the Fort Impracticable and the Fort Artselmo, the former belonging to our rivals, and the latter being the stronghold or keep on our side.

Being the more conversant with our fort, it will not be amiss to give a description of it. The Fort Anselmo was ninety-five yards in circumference at this sandy spot. A few pine trees were felled and others growing in a natural circle; and between the intervals of these trees large holes were dug in the sand, into which the stems of small pine trees were buried and the holes filled up. To these props the wickerwork was interwoven and made fast to the trunks of the trees which formed the circle. The wickerwork enclosure being finished and of great strength, was interwoven with evergreens of broad and expansive leaf; a sandbank within was raised about three feet, as a sort of rampart, and to add to the durability of the stakes and the fence, which was seven feet high, and when standing on the raised parapet within, it was about breast high, to enable us to pour down pine-tops on any assailants who should attempt to take the fort by escalade, for ladders were actually manufactured during our warfare for such purposes, and at every four or five yards there were piles of pine-tops, after the manner of cannon-balls on the ramparts of more scientific fortresses.

Without this wickerwork fence was a dry ditch three feet deep and four in breadth, and all this labour was resorted to for amusement, as well as to keep out the alligators or other noxious animals and reptiles from paying us nocturnal visits. Within this strong enclosure were two tents and two huts, the latter constructed with such care as to rival the most fanciful grottos, formed at great cost and time; and near the middle of the sandy space which was carefully swept with brooms made from the smaller shrubs, was a large rude table chiselled with rough-edged tools; the stools or seats were of the same rough workmanship and un-carpenter-like finish. This rough and ready table, and the seats enclosing it, were not moveable or fixed upon fashionable castors; quite the contrary, they were nailed to the stumps and stems of decapitated trees, and in truth, might be called the fixtures of the tempest, for there they stood in rough outlines defying the pattering of the rain, or the unceremonious tempest strong, stiff, and sturdy, and even capable of bearing a heavier weight of viands than these times of scarcity afforded.

This broad and coarse fixture deigned not to groan or to grow rickety under the weight of intemperance, and around this board sat seven voyagers, moustached, and clothed in tarnished scarlet uniforms. One wore an hussar *pelisse*; another was adorned with a satin waistcoat, richly embroidered, and studded with glass to represent precious stones, brought from Rodrigo in Spain; another nourished a silver fork wanting one prong, which he brought from Badajoz, and which had dived into many a garlic dish, or been stuck into the mutton of Spanish Estremadura, or had played its part in the capital of Old Spain, and now flourished in the New World, employed in carrying helpless oysters to the same mouth and lips which bargained for it at one half of its intrinsic value; and Benjamin Smith, a worthy soldier, might be seen caressing a pretty little parakeet, which had just recovered from a slight wound in the wing that had brought it from the bough of an adjacent tree. A few days after this interesting little bird of green plumage was made captive, it would run of a morning to visit the different mattresses which lay on the ground, and would nestle under the clothes apparently with the greatest transports of delight.

In this inclosure, so famed for oyster feasts, pickled veal, and rushy-flavoured beef, which was all carefully stowed away in smuggled casks, containing salt brine which formerly held lumps of junk, we made merry over our cups, the great fire blazing brightly, and the rosin flaring in gas-like flames from the logs of the pine. This place, of a night, more resembled the resort of *banditti* than the abode of officers once so starched, stiff, and erect on England's parade-ground.

Shooting was the order of the day; few went abroad without a firelock or fowling-piece both for sport and self-protection against the prolific produce of this, I may say, living soil, infested with creeping and strange animals, buzzing flies, and searching mosquitoes; the trees were alive with birds; many of their screaming notes were shrill and piercing. Every few yards some bird flew past, or perched on a distant bough, all presenting tempting objects for the marksman. But unluckily we lacked of small shot; some spent whole days in cutting leaden bullets into small lumps or particles, and others, more scientifically inclined, endeavoured to turn manufacturers of shot.

One invention totally failed, and the inventor, while boring holes in the bottom of an old tin kettle with laudable and philosophical patience, flattered himself that all his hopes would be crowned with complete success. The supposed necessary number of punctures being finished, a quantity of leaden bullets were melted down, the holey tin cover was held over a cask of water, and the important experiment began; the molten lead was poured on the tin cover; certainly a few drops of lead fell through the holes into the water, but they only presented a few misshapen lumps. But here the mishap and failure did not end, for, ere the operator and the inventor could get breath, all the holes in the tin kettle were plugged up with lead, and his whole day's labour was soldered up as it were in half a minute. After this I saw no more attempts at the manufacturing of small shot.

In the middle of the arena of Fort Anselmo was a slender pine tree, lopped of its branches, from the top of which waved a flag of two colours, composed of white and blue silk, emblematical of the facings of the Royal Fusiliers and the forty-third Light Infantry.

Our soldiers (servants) were hutted in an outwork, without the principal gate of the fort; under the archway was a square hole of considerable depth, over which beams were laid as a sort of drawbridge, which could be displaced at pleasure, so that the alligators might here be foiled in their attempts at crawling into the fort. Round the servants' huts was another dry sandy ditch with an embankment or parapet; this place was called the parade-ground; at the corner of it we had sunk a well, the water of which, like the rest in this island, was of brackish taste, like the water drunk at many of the spas by English invalids, as a cleanser after the joys of the table; however, as this was the best water to be got, we were obliged to put up with its spa-like taste morning, noon, and night, yet I cannot say that all of us did not enjoy the most robust and vigorous health, eating and drinking our coarse fare under the concave of etherial blue, heedless which way the wind blew.

At the back of this fort there was a small wickerwork door wove with curious ingenuity, and just large enough for admitting one person at a time, by climbing out of the ditch; and the branched exterior of this small outlet so exactly corresponded with the exterior wickerwork fence, that it was totally impossible to detect that such an outlet existed: and this secret aperture was unknown to any of us, save one who was the planner of it, and this ingenious handicraftsman had laboured at its construction behind his own hut, and for more than a month he went and came by it; we often wondered how he disappeared from the fort when he was often seen only to enter his own hut, and frequently voices called him from the ill-shapen and unpolished board of hilarity, and even some went in search of him, as there was no answer returned, but he was no where to be found. In the end this small doorway saved Fort Anselmo from capture in the day of strife—nay, another half-minute's delay would have deprived its possessors of it, and the silken colours of blue and white would have been torn down, and have formed a trophy and been most likely suspended beneath the flag of yellow and green of our opponents, the champions of the Fort Impracticable.

Before the fusiliers had joined us, I assembled the officers of our own corps only, and moved into the open space for the purpose of bringing the eight-fifth and the rifle-corps to action in the open plain, mustering about equal numbers with our opponents. But they would not come forth from the cover of their entrenchments, and amused my advanced guard by giving them some stray shots, and a good deal of desultory skirmishing took place. As commander, I was stationary with my main body two hundred yards behind all, out of reach of the enemy's projectiles, and surrounded by my main body, ready to succour at those points where the hottest of the action raged.

While looking eagerly towards the flanks, I all at once caught a glimpse of the Scotch caps of the ninety-third Highlanders gliding through the woods, and who were absolutely marching in such a direction as would force me to show two faces, or rather to throw my adherents on two sides of a square. Although the ninety-third had not declared against us, still I thought precautionary measures necessary, and I ordered my vanguard to retire slowly; if followed, to continue to fight in retreat, but, if possible, to conceal from their opponents that a retrograde movement was decided upon across a plain and in front of three regiments against us. This retrograde movement being adopted with all the regularity and good conduct desired by my most sanguine wishes, I immediately, unknown to any except my second in command, quitted the field, leaving him to continue the action until my return; at full stretch of legs I ran to the portals of the Fort Anselmo, ordered the bridge to be taken up, leaving only one person as sentinel at its gate, and then caused great heaps of pine-tops to be conveyed to a position at the edge of the wood, where I resolved to fight at all hazards, although against such odds.

After a brave struggle my army was completely routed,

and the greater part prostrate and taken prisoners. The enemy were two to one in the encounter, and as all small bodies, when once broken, are generally annihilated, this was the case with us after one hour's fighting; a few of the right wing only saved themselves by diving through the thicket, to endeavour to regain Fort Anselmo by the secret entrance, and there enter, if possible, to man the ramparts and to save the fort.

Only one individual from my centre and left, during the hot pursuit, contrived to reach the outworks in front of the principal entrance of Fort Anselmo, and that was Don Sebastian, of dark visage, made still darker by the contusions he had received in the fray; thus breathless and alone, without his cap, he stood, the picture of everything that was delightful—the sole champion to repel a host, who then jumped into the ditch to climb the banks of the outwork, and to grapple with the only defender, who was of strong arm, redoubtable, and of a chivalric spirit, and withal of deep romance. Whether he was inspired at the legendary tales of the old women and nurses of the Highlands, or whether the deeds of the most redoubtable chieftains of his ancestors had fired his brain, I know not. But he was a host, and well-nigh beggared and set at nought the mighty and tough legends of old, when knights with battle-axe or ponderous sword, uplifted with both hands, clove in twain the sculls of all comers; for as the climbers mounted to the assault, he tumbled them into the little fosse one after the other; but at length waxing feeble with long turmoil, he was overpowered, and thrown headlong by many hands into the ditch.

Lieutenant Gleig, of the eighty-fifth, headed this party most valiantly, and I must say he spared no endeavours to take the fort. With his own hands he tore down the colours of Fort Anselmo, and under a shower of pine-tops boldly sprung towards the entrance, and finding the bridge gone, unhesitatingly jumped into the hole under the gateway; but here he was entrapped and met his fate. Lieutenant Steele, a Yorkshireman, seized hold of him and obliged him to surrender himself a prisoner in the very place which he had intended to leave with trophies and as a conqueror.

There stood the festooned wickerwork portals invitingly open; but others of his partisan allies, running the gauntlet, and eager for the capture of this fort, sprung into the ditch, and peeping into the wide-gaping sand-pit, they unhesitatingly flew from its tottering brink, and carrying with them the ocular tidings of its great depth to their main body, they all hesitated, and came to a stand-still, and by way of gaining time and recovering from their sudden panic they sent forward to demand the surrender of the fortress; but the only signal they obtained from the skeleton remains of its defenders, was a bold front from their lofty breastworks, pointing in derision to the open portals and the sand-pit under its archway.

The partisan allies tenaciously clung to the parade-ground or outworks of the fort; but finding as they cooled, after the fray, that their contusions began to be painful, they were glad to enter into a treaty, wherein the garrison demanded my release, and that I should negotiate the following protocol:

Fort Anselmo
The inner part belongs to the forces of Anselmo, the outworks to the enemy, who are to immediately occupy them. It is agreed that in three parts of an hour the enemy's forces are to be in the works taken. But if not occupied by them in the stated time, General Anselmo's forces are to take possession of them.
(Signed) *Anselmo*
Commander-in-Chief
N. C. Travers
Com.

And here follows the exact copy, word for word, which I wrote at the time in my defence of the late battle, to show that our rivals brought into the field (against all the rules of war ancient or modern,) other partisan allies, who had not previously taken either directly or indirectly any share in the petty warfare, but by stealth had crept through a wood, and come over its borders, had attacked the left and threatened the rear of my adherents, without even sending a herald to announce to which side they were about to proffer their assistance; however, I thought it more glorious to fight with fourteen men against twenty-eight than to retire, there being some honour in winning the day, and little discredit in losing it. Hutchinson and Lorentz, of the Royal Fusiliers, seeing the disparity of numbers, joined us, and we were more than once within an ace of winning the day.

Anselmo Castle
Dauphin Island
In the morning I perceived the enemy drawn up in heavy columns on the high road leading to their entrenchments in order of battle. I immediately ordered General Considine to move on with the first brigade of his division to reconnoitre them, which he did to my satisfaction after some slight skirmishing, and drove the enemy's pickets close in to their main body. Seeing this, I determined to move on with my whole army, and defeat them before any reinforcements could arrive. The first brigade of the light division was at this time hotly engaged, and gained some partial advantages, though against a superior body. At this time I perceived the ninety-third army moving through the wood with an evident intention to turn my left, (though war had not been declared against that nation.) This movement determined me to fall back and take up a position in

a wood in front of Anselmo Castle, which I did with some loss, as the enemy continued pushing on in a determined manner, intending if possible to bring me to action in the plain, which I was determined to avoid if possible, as the army was double mine in numbers. I had just got my troops into position, when the enemy made a most determined charge on my centre, resting on the high road to Anselmo. At the same time they attempted to turn my right. In both these attacks they were repulsed by the gallantry of my troops.

My right was severely engaged under General Steele; several attacks were renewed on my left and centre, but failed where I commanded in person. The enemy then made a flank movement towards my left, where I immediately went, leaving Generals Considine and MacLean, senior, who were bravely repelling the enemy in the centre. At this time, by the superior force of the enemy, notwithstanding all my efforts, he succeeded in turning my left, under Field-Marshal Travers in person, whom, as well as a colonel of the ninety-third, I made prisoners, when their reserve came up, dispersed and routed the third division, released the prisoners I had made, and took me while I was endeavouring to get Marshal Travers away.

General Considine, finding his rear threatened, commenced his retreat, disputing every inch of ground. Unfortunately he exposed himself too much and was made prisoner, when the army, seeing this, was in much confusion. General MacLean continued the action, and rallied the army at the outworks of Anselmo, where, after a most desperate effort to restore the fortune of the day, this general was also taken prisoner.

The enemy then assaulted the castle, commanded by Deputy Governors Steele and Madden, and were repulsed with the loss of some prisoners.

Other skirmishes and affairs took place, and I afterwards made an attempt to take Fort Impracticable with the united forces of the Royal Fusiliers and the officers of the dismounted squadron of the fourteenth Light Dragoons, but failed, owing to the fortieth regiment attacking us before a declaration of war, as the ninety-third had done. Our rivals had dug a deep pit within the open doorway of their fort, similar to the sandpit beneath the portals of our fort. Penrice, of the fusiliers, was entrapped in the hole of their sand-pit.

Herewith follow extracts of more despatches which fell into my hands.

Headquarters of the Eighty-fifth Forces.

Sir,—In answer to your despatch, which I have received by your aid-de-camp, I beg leave to inform you that what you have mentioned with respect to the seventh regiment is on our part agreed to; but as you state yourselves and the seventh to be independent nations, we consider ourselves, the fortieth and ninety-third, in the same light: we have therefore made the same proposals to them which you have to the seventh.

The articles which you propose in your despatches we fully agree to, except that part which alludes to the half-hour's notice previous to any attack being made. It is our fixed determination to attack at any moment after the stipulated hour which may suit our convenience; and the only weapon with which we shall expect to meet is the *pineapple.*

No fences shall on any account be broken down or entered except where a breach or gateway is apparent, or by scaling.
By order of the Commander of the Forces,
G. I. Watts
Military Secretary

To Gen. Considine

Commanding advance of the forty-third
Sir,—I have just received this note, and send it for your perusal. You will perceive they will not agree to give notice of an attack. I think they mean to endeavour to surprise us. If you have any orders send to me, and I will make arrangements, and give out general orders about the divisions providing themselves with ammunition, havresacks, &c. &c.

Will you appoint my division, or shall I do it?—What strength must it be?
James Considine
Gen. Advance

To His Excellency Don Anselmo
Commander-in- Chief

The suspicion conveyed in the last document, that a surprise was in contemplation by our opponents, was not given at random, for a few nights after the receipt of it, the writer of the first of these documents was detected in the uniform of a private soldier, and made captive in the very act of taking the depth of the dry ditch of our out-works, which had been recently strengthened.

A naval aide-de-camp, one day, somehow contrived to get hold of an animal carrying the framework of a horse, and, with lance in hand, this nautical personage came in front of our fort as a herald of defiance. Having examined from withinside the outlines of himself and steed, and seeing as we did that his seat was what may be termed only a loose hold of the saddle, it was agreed amongst us as we parleyed with him, that the most fleet of foot, with pine-top in hand, should go forth and make a prize of this horse and its rider.

But not to do an injustice to this maritime officer on horseback, away from his own element, and the land of lubbers, I must state that, like a good *vidette,* as soon as he saw himself likely to be beset on such an unwieldy beast of bad provender, he made a most desperate effort to swing round, pulling and seesawing away at the bridle, with hands wide asunder, and at the same time most unmercifully pounding the animal's ribs and belly which sounded like an old drum. But in truth the animal had no go in it, and the tack was only half completed when he missed stays; the pedestrian came up, and laying hold of one of the rider's nautical feet, lifted him from the centre of gravity, and gave him of the blue jacket a most complete capsize; and so straightened were we for the fresh solids, that it was rather dubious whether the old horse (had it not been too tough a *morceau*) would not have been cut into chunks, clapped into the pickling-tub, and thus shared a like fate to the admiral's milch cow.

The captive horse-sailor, in perfect good humour, and his steed, were conveyed into our little fort, and the unresisting horse was tied to a tree. Its rider, after brushing the dust off, and being seated at our rough board, was reminded by his land-captor that some few years before, when he of the red cloth first went on board of a man-of-war, like a maritime soldier, being ill at ease from the tossing and bounding motion of the sea rocking-horse, which put his stomach in bad order, and while heaving up its contents, the middies dangled before his eyes fat pork, and threatened to swab him by day, while at the midnight hour they opened the middle seams of his close-fitting hammock, out of which he fell on the deck in his blanket, whence, extricating himself from its folds, he crawled he knew not whither, his only covering consisting of his short linen garment, and in this way scrambling about, he at last cast anchor on the damp cabletier, until relieved by an old quarter-master with a lantern and candle.

But our petty warfare was now about to finish, to give place to the comic muse; and before I close this subject, I can only say that I did not know a single instance of any angry feeling or an ill word having passed between the champions of either side, although some sorely battered heads were the result of these vigorous encounters, out of which sprung the foregoing despatches, the spontaneous effusions of unsophisticated subalterns.

Lieutenant Wyms, of the royal navy, and an officer of our corps, planned and marked out a piece of ground for the intended erection of a pastoral theatre, at the back of our encampment, where four erect pine trees grew, which were by nature placed in such a convenient manner, that by the decapitation of other trees of irregular growth, and clearing away the underwood, the above four trees were so exactly opposite one another at a given distance (both as to the wished-for breadth and length of the intended erection), that they formed the angles and the four corners of the gable ends of the contemplated transatlantic place of amusement. Holes were then dug a few feet apart, between the open spaces of these four trees, into which the stems of other pine trees, lopped of their tufted branches, were deeply sunken, and made to stand erect without support by re-filling the holes, and then with hand-piles pounding down the earth into a hard substance.

The main framework being thus established upon a sufficient and solid basis for the purpose for which it was intended, the entanglement of the wickerwork was begun, and the boughs and branches of trees were interwoven and twisted together with indefatigable labour and exactitude, well worthy of the old trade of basket-making. This wickerwork was raised to the height of thirty feet, and formed the sides, the back, and the front of this construction, which was about sixty feet in length, and thirty in breadth; the top being covered over with the canvass or the main-sails from the men-of-war, which also supplied ship-carpenters and sawyers for the purpose of cutting planks for the stage, to form the orchestra and the seats for the accommodation of the audience.

The canvass for the scenery and the oil-colours were also supplied from the fleet, and several officers assisted in throwing in the lights and shades of the scenery for stage-effect.

At this moment, when in want of spangled finery, a cargo of trans-atlantic comedinas were made captives by an English cruiser, while on their passage from some islands to the main. Of these harmless people we saw nothing, and indeed heard they were set at liberty; but their garments were withheld, and these flimsy green-room dresses of transparent texture of male and female attire were deposited in bundles in the Isle Dauphin, as a most seasonable supply for the amateurs, who were in ecstasies at such an unlooked-for selection of gaudy stuffs, being, as it were, cast on the island, and all ready made for both sexes, or, more properly speaking, for the transmogrifying of males into the flounces and other female trappings—our camp, as it may be supposed, being ill supplied with characters for the feminine parts.

These dresses being spread out to dry, were like so many bunting signal-flags, and as occasion required they were served out to the expectant amateurs, who were about to figure away in the comedy of *The Honeymoon*, and the after-piece of *The Mayor of Garret*. In the comedy Captain West, of the Royal Engineers, was most excellent, and when ordered to swallow all his own pills, he said, "Oh, one's a dose."

Both pieces went off with most exceedingly great *eclat*, in the presence of a numerous audience of united naval and military spectators.

An officer of our regiment was detached to an adjacent island, and as the weather was exceedingly fine in March, two of us set sail in a small boat without a compass, but more by good fortune than management. The weather remained clear, and when half way across we observed two or three sandy islands nearly covered with hundreds of white pelicans, which sailed off in three distinct bodies, sending out flankers on every side. Although we fired several bullets, we did not succeed in killing one of them. These birds are exceedingly wild, and very hard to be approached.

The following evening we saw a boat decorated with flags, and the music playing the American national air, and on our return we heard that peace was proclaimed, or in course of adjustment. From this time provisions and wines of all kinds poured in from all quarters; from the most frugal and parsimonious meals, and the utmost scarcity, every luxury was had that could be procured; fish were caught by hundreds, and there was a good supply of bread, (the oysters made excellent sauce,) for without this staff of life the choicest viands cannot be enjoyed. A ship brought a cargo of the best ale I ever remember drinking.

But as if some torment was always forthcoming in these hemispheres, the mosquitoes began to bite most terrifically, and while shooting in the marshes and swamps they would pierce through the trousers, and by the time we got on board ship to return to England my eyes were nearly closed, and my skin in a perfect state of inflammation. How it was

I know not, but these tormenting flies seemed particularly fond of probing my veins, and I did not see anyone so plagued with them as myself; they were of a very large species—indeed everything in this part of the world seemed to flourish and grow to a great size—the centipedes are as large as my little finger.

Mobile Bay was a good deal intersected with sandbanks, and that part of the wooded island of L'Isle Dauphin, opposite Mobile Bay, was also fringed with sandbanks, which gave it a lively appearance in comparison with the wretched flat coasts along which we had sailed. The oysters which we obtained in such abundance were gathered on the opposite side of this flat island, and were usually brought for our consumption by fatigue parties in sacks; there was also a sort of small tree that grew on the island, the leaves of which, when boiled, made a drink possessing a very agreeable flavour, and while we were in want of tea made an excellent substitute.

During the latter part of our two months' stay at this place a supply of flour reached us, and ovens were erected for baking bread. The first loaf made was sent as a present to our mess, weighing eight pounds, the top of it being stamped with the words "To the Bang-up Mess" including Madden, Steele, Houlton, Considine, MacLean and myself, and counting a certain number of battles that each of us had been engaged in, amounting in the gross, or clubbed together, to forty-three pitched battles, besides skirmishes and other affairs, with a share of nine wounds or "hits," as they were technically called. Our united ages (all being very young men) amounted to a hundred and thirty-three years, and we measured, taking one with the other, thirty-five feet ten inches.

CHAPTER 14

Voyage to England

On the 8th of April our regiment, with the seven fusiliers, set sail for England, but experiencing calms and baffling winds in the gulf of Mexico, we did not reach the mouth of the harbour of Havana, the capital of the island of Cuba, for a fortnight; and as six months had passed without our seeing a town or a village, it was with considerable pleasure we heard that we were about to enter the harbour, as most of the ships were denied that piece of good fortune, and were under the necessity of making a long passage home on salt provisions, or the few articles laid in at L'Isle Dauphin.

The channel of the harbour of the city of Havana is very narrow; to the left, on entering, stands the castle of the Moro, frowning defiance on a rock, and overlooking the extensive city which stands on flat ground at the water's edge on the opposite side of the harbour, (commanded by the Moro,) is encircled by fortifications, but of no great strength beyond the town. Inland the harbour widens, and was filled by hulks and men-of-war lying in ordinary; altogether it very much in shape resembles the Hamoaze river, that passes Devonport in England. Here it is that some of the finest ships in the Spanish navy have been built. As it was late in the evening before we let go our anchor, we did not land until the following morning, which broke with a clear sky and hot sun.

The principal inhabitants of this place are Spaniards, or of Spanish extraction, adopting the dress and manners of the mother-country. The troops are Spaniards, but the great mass of the population consist of *creoles, mulattoes,* and every shade and cast of colour from the *black* to the *yellow,* or *saffron-coloured,* commonly called *white,* so that out of six or seven people promenading, each possesses a different cast of complexion, or claims a peculiar line of ancestry, which of course brings them back to crosses and counter-crosses, of all the wicked amours so often practiced, where people of various colours and nations amalgamate.

Havana being so famous for its cigars, we had the curiosity to enter a warehouse to see the process of making them: the ragged edge of the tobacco leaf is cut off with a knife, twirled in a small lump, and the leaf rolled round it and twisted at each end with the fingers, and it is surprising with what celerity and dexterity they are made, lighted, and smoked. The mildest tobacco is put into small white papers, under the name of *ladies' cigars,* who commonly use them. I have also seen actresses in Spain smoking this kind of cigars while rehearsing their parts, but in the mother-country they are not so commonly used by the *señoras* as in this colony.

In the afternoon crowds of people were issuing from the city, in *volantes* or *cabriolets,* on mules and on foot, to a circus half a mile without the walls, where we followed, and as it was broad daylight when the exhibition of horsemanship commenced, we had a full opportunity of examining the motley crowds of black, brown, yellow, copper, and lead colour, with innumerable large black eyes, refulgently sparkling, and shooting forth a wild expression of kindness towards the strangers of fairer complexion, clothed in lively uniforms. The exhibition opened according to the Spanish fashion, by a group of mounted *caballeros,* gaily caparisoned, going through a variety of intricate evolutions with admirable exactness and precision, and altogether the riding was of a very superior description.

The next day we visited the theatre, which was fitted up in good style, and as large as our minor theatres; but as there was no performance while the circus was open, we had not an opportunity of judging of the merits of the performers.

The market is exceedingly well supplied with poultry, pigs, yams, cocoanuts and pineapples, which are piled up in heaps, with various other delicious fruits and vegetables. The market women are mostly negresses, and certainly some of the most hideous creatures possessing the human form I ever beheld, not excepting the savages. Some of these black women were enormously fat, and sat on the ground with their legs wide open, a loose robe only being girded round the middle; they were sweating and shining to such a degree that they looked as if greased all over with hogs lard, and the wool on the old negresses' heads was quite grey, which, together with their broad flat nostrils, thick lips, enormous mouths, and sooty visages, gave them an appearance such as we have pictured to our imaginations of hobgoblins, or a species of monster to scare civilized generations.

The negroes are by far the finest and most athletic race of blacks I ever beheld, and assume and practice an air of independence in imitation of the Spanish *dons,* which, in addition to their low craft and cunning, makes them also the most insolent set of fellows to be imagined: and, as a proof of this assertion, I must recount a trick of familiarity which might have been the least anticipated from a slave towards strange officers.

Some of the fusiliers and our officers were walking together, seven in number, when up came a negro, making a most gracious bow, saying, in a garbled mixture of Spanish and English, *"Caballeros—I know pretty lady—seben pretty daughters—live in handsome house—out the walls—señora too proud—see noble strangers—with coffee, music también;"* a proposal we assented to with one accord, as he proffered us his safe conduct to the house—nay, we even fancied he had been sent expressly to waylay us by some party who had lost their hearts at the circus the night before, and our only fears were that a sufficiency of vehicles could not be obtained to convey us to so charming a party, having no doubt of a speedy admission, for I must premise that all the doors of the houses (which are stained of various colours) were left wide open, to admit a free current of air to pass through the corridors to keep them cool, for the heat now was equal to *las dios de canucarales,* or the dog-days in England. Our suspense was of short duration, for the black acquitted himself to perfection and brought three *cabriolets,* stuck upon lofty wheels, which we entered, and our guide placed himself behind one of them, and off we whirled at a rattling pace. At the expiration of half an hour's rapid driving, up one street and down another, we began to inquire how much further we had to go. The drivers pretended to be bewildered, and calling to the guide he was nowhere to be found. The drivers drew up and demanded an exorbitant fare; and the height of the joke was, that we found out we were on the identical spot whence we had started, that is to say, in the middle of the city. Expostulations would have been useless, it being evident that these people were all in league; therefore, with a hearty laugh, we acquiesced in the cheatery.

The posados, or lemonade-houses, were crowded with Spaniards smoking *cigars* or quaffing the juice of the lime out of pint tumblers; and having partaken of this refreshing beverage, we strolled towards the Alameda, a promenade close to the harbour, where prattling groups of señoras fantastically glided up and down until midnight. The pale rays of the moon reflected on the water such scenes as these indelibly fix on the memory—these tranquil hours which float in recollection, as having occurred at some period of our lives in strange hemispheres.

At sunrise the following morning we sailed out of the harbour with the morning breeze; in the evening the wind blows into the harbour, and in a contrary direction of a morning, at least so we were informed, and so it happened with us. At this early hour numbers of females of every shade and colour were flocking down the shore to bathe in *publico,* and in a perfect state of nudity: many of the negresses of *en bon point* before and behind, with their long heels, looked mighty ridiculous.

The day before, a plentiful stock of every sort of provisions had been purchased, but the cargo of fruit, as ordered, had not arrived, and when a mile out at sea, a small vessel, crowding all sail, made towards us. We hove to; but on its coming up, the owner protested, with vehement Spanish gesticulations, that we were not the officers who had ordered the fruit. His anger, however, was somewhat appeased when it was intimated to him that he would have to take it back unless all despatch was used in putting his cargo on board at his own price, which he consented to, and an abundant store of oranges, pincapples, limes, jars of sweetmeats and preserves of the sweetest and the most delicious flavour, were heaped on the deck in such profusion as to create great difficulty in stowing them away. Pineapples in clusters adorned every corner of the cabin, and an extensive netting just above the stern-windows was almost breaking down with the weight of oranges.

The wind was favourable while passing the Gulf stream; but soon after we got into a tempestuous ocean, and were tossed about at the mercy of the mighty element, with dead lights in the cabin windows, for some days. The convoy were separated and were scattered over the face of the waters, and running before the wind almost under bare poles, in three successive days, according to the reckoning we made, a distance of seven hundred and twenty miles; and as the sea-chart lay on the table marked with pencil, we traced our homeward course with great satisfaction: and, as far as I can judge, the sailors invariably look out for port with little less glee than a landsman.

Our accommodation on board the frigate was of the most superior order: the spacious wardroom was given up for the sole occupation of ten officers, the few naval officers taking up their berths in the gun-room, and the captain resided in a cabin constructed on the main deck.

The provisions were in abundance: ducks, turkeys, or fresh meat daily stood on the table, the wine went round without limitation, and the choicest fruits formed our dessert. Hot rolls were served up for breakfast every morning; and I can aver, from the time we left Havana, that I had hardly crunched biscuit. Many amateurs like biscuit; but we had seen such myriads of it, that a crust of bread was always preferred.

During the voyage two immense turtles were caught, one weighing one hundred and sixty pounds; a fine large grey pelican, which had been disabled by shot at L'Isle Dauphin, only lived half the passage on lairs of fat pork, and at length died, as fish could not be procured for its support. In this way, with foul or fair weather, we stood off Land's End, old England in view, with countless white sails decorating the surface of the water. What a sight for the mariner! What an association of ideas does it not call forth!

A small vessel hove to and sent newspapers on board.

Was it credible? Did our eyes deceive us, or was everything turned topsy-turvy? For behold, long columns of type recounted Napoleon's invasion of France from the Isle of Elba, in four vessels carrying eight hundred infantry and one hundred Polish dragoons, to recover the imperial diadem, in the face of all Europe, while her plenipotentiaries were assembled at Vienna.

What a march! Who will attempt to describe a march? Snails crawl; here was a power enlarging in magnitude, still increasing, and threatening to crush and grind to powder all who attempted to oppose its irresistible progress. Every effort succumbed or was swept away in the vortex, and the delirium which pervaded all classes sufficed, by a bloodless conquest, and without a blow. The reins of government were once more placed in the hands of Napoleon, and the legitimate King of France was exiled from his dominions.

War, interminable war! Europe flew to arms. The alarm spread like wildfire; nay, farther, even the Calmuc Tartars were put into request. The British Channel presented a busy scene; and the naval and military establishments of England, her men-of-war on land and afloat, were put into requisition, at a ruinous cost, to stem the torrent once more about to overflow and devastate Europe's fair fields.

In this state of affairs the *Bucephalus* frigate, armed *en flute* from her transatlantic voyage, let go her anchor at Spithead on the 1st of June; the transports, being less fortunate, were still struggling against the blasts amid the floating icebergs on the banks of Newfoundland.

Two days of respite were allowed at Portsmouth, which we quitted without a pang. The breeze was favourable, the day lovely, the sky clear, our stomachs in good order to partake of fresh vegetables and provisions, happy mariners, gliding on the tranquil waters within hail of Brighton's cliffs and shingled shores, and our band of music playing Spanish *boleros*.

When I was a boy, Brighton was a little town; and I can never obliterate from my memory the transports of delight, and the joy felt by my youthful mind, while crossing its sunburnt downs covered with large bodies of troops, and at the firing of their cannon at a grand review; my first glimpse of the gilded dolphin on the towers of the old church; the polished tiles and bricks of the houses shining in the noon-day sun; the brown sod of the open Steine covered with fishermen's nets; a bluff bystander exclaiming, looking towards the nets, "Yonder be cop-tin, with the silver ring on—he's got two fishing-boats and a punt" But a truce to the days of boyhood; I bad now reached man's estate, and must not forget that I was on board His Majesty's *Bucephalus*, sweeping along coastwise.

The gentle zephyrs continued, and the vessel rippling through the tiny waves, we skimmed our course past the chalky cliffs of Dover, landed at Deal, whence we marched back to Dover and took possession of its venerable castle, where we found a strong draft of soldiers from the second battalion awaiting our arrival. In a few days the remainder of the regiment had disembarked from the transports; on the 16th of June we were all put on board small craft for the purpose of joining the allied armies in the Netherlands, and in the evening we left the harbour under easy sail for Ostend amid the acclamations of the people.

LEONAUR

ALSO FROM LEONAUR

AVAILABLE IN SOFTCOVER OR HARDCOVER WITH DUST JACKET

SEPOYS, SIEGE & STORM by *Charles John Griffiths*—The Experiences of a young officer of H.M.'s 61st Regiment at Ferozepore, Delhi ridge and at the fall of Delhi during the Indian mutiny 1857.

CAMPAIGNING IN ZULULAND by *W. E. Montague*—Experiences on campaign during the Zulu war of 1879 with the 94th Regiment.

THE STORY OF THE GUIDES by *G. J. Younghusband*—The Exploits of the Soldiers of the famous Indian Army Regiment from the northwest frontier 1847 - 1900..

ZULU: 1879 by *D.C.F. Moodie & the Leonaur Editors*—The Anglo-Zulu War of 1879 from contemporary sources: First Hand Accounts, Interviews, Dispatches, Official Documents & Newspaper Reports.

THE RECOLLECTIONS OF SKINNER OF SKINNER'S HORSE by *James Skinner*—James Skinner and his 'Yellow Boys' Irregular cavalry in the wars of India between the British, Mahratta, Rajput, Mogul, Sikh & Pindarree Forces.

TOMMY ATKINS' WAR STORIES 14 FIRST HAND ACCOUNTS—Fourteen first hand accounts from the ranks of the British Army during Queen Victoria's Empire Original & True Battle Stories Recollections of the Indian Mutiny With the 49th in the Crimea With the Guards in Egypt The Charge of the Six Hundred With Wolseley in Ashanti Alma, Inkermann and Magdala With the Gunners at Tel-el-Kebir Russian Guns and Indian Rebels Rough Work in the Crimea In the Maori Rising Facing the Zulus From Sebastopol to Lucknow Sent to Save Gordon On the March to Chitral Tommy by Rudyard Kipling

CHASSEUR OF 1914 by *Marcel Dupont*—Experiences of the twilight of the French Light Cavalry by a young officer during the early battles of the great war in Europe.

TROOP HORSE & TRENCH by *R. A. Lloyd*—The experiences of a British Lifeguardsman of the household cavalry fighting on the western front during the First World War 1914-18.

THE EAST AFRICAN MOUNTED RIFLES by *C. J. Wilson*—Experiences of the campaign in the East African bush during the First World War.

THE FIGHTING CAMELIERS by *Frank Reid*—The exploits of the Imperial Camel Corps in the desert and Palestine campaigns of the First World War.

www.ingramcontent.com/pod-product-compliance
Lightning Source LLC
Chambersburg PA
CBHW021104090426
42738CB00006B/490